MW01679542

GETTING PAID IN FULL

W. Kelsea Wilber

Small Business Sourcebooks
from
Sourcebooks, Inc.
Naperville, Illinois

Published by: **Sourcebooks Trade**
A Division of Sourcebooks, Inc.
P.O. Box 372, Naperville, Illinois, 60566
(708) 961-3900
FAX: 708-961-2168

Editorial: John Santucci
Cover Design: Wayne Johnson/Dominique Raccah
Interior Design and Production: Wayne Johnson, Sourcebooks, Inc.

This publication is designed to provide accurate and authoritative information in regard to the subject matter covered. It is sold with the understanding that the publisher is not engaged in rendering legal, accounting, or other professional service. If legal advice or other expert assistance is required, the services of a competent professional person should be sought.

From a Declaration of Principles Jointly Adopted by a Committee of the American Bar Association and a Committee of Publishers and Associations

Library of Congress Cataloging-in-Publication Data

Wlber, Wanda K.

Getting paid in full : collect the money you are owed and develop a successful credit policy / W. Kelsea Wilber.
p. cm.
Includes index.
ISBN 0-942061-71-3 : $17.95. -- ISBN 0-942061-68-3 (pbk.) : $8.95
1. Collection of accounts. 2. Credit—Management. 3. Small business—Finance. I. Title.
HG3752.5.W54 1994
658.8'8--dc20 93-31316
CIP

Printed and bound in the United States of America.
Hardcover--10 9 8 7 6 5 4 3 2 1
Paperback--10 9 8 7 6 5 4 3 2 1

Table of Contents

About The Author

W. Kelsea Wilber is a writer and an attorney in private practice. She is licensed to practice in Illinois and Florida. Her law practice is concentrated in collection and international business trading and consulting.

She has published *The Illinois Legal Filing Directory, 1990, 1991, 1992,* Shepards-McGraw Hill, Colorado Springs, CO; *Small Claims Court Without a Lawyer,* 1991, Financial Sourcebooks, Naperville, IL; *How to Form Your Own Corporation,* 1993, Sphinx Publishing, Clearwater, FL; and *Lawsuits of the Rich and Famous,* to be published in May, 1994 by Sphinx Publishing, Clearwater, FL.

Acknowledgements

This book would not have been possible without the inspiration and encouragement of my father and friend, Donald L. Wilber, Esq. He could have written the book, but he let me do it instead.

My thanks to all the members of my family who gave such terrific assistance along the way.

Preface

The purpose of this book is to assist professionals and small business owners in collecting accounts receivable. For those with no effective experience, it is designed to provide an understanding of techniques that work and how to use them. For those with experience, this book allows them to turn to a specific chapter in order to educate themselves on more advanced techniques, refresh their memories, and learn a new skill.

This is a "how to" book that explains how to proceed on a step-by-step basis. It will help the small business owner develop practices that maximize the collection of accounts current and past due. This book can help you collect money from customers who will not pay on time and from those who do not want to pay at all.

Every dollar collected on your receivable accounts goes directly toward improving your bottom line. For many professionals and small business owners, uncollected accounts receivable represent a significant potential asset. For the cash basis business, these accounts are not considered taxable income. For the accrual basis business, the accounts are income and are on the balance sheet, but are usually highly qualified in the accounting footnotes. In both cases, most financial institutions are very reluctant to give credit based on accounts receivable.

Preface

If goods are not paid for when delivered or services when rendered, credit has been extended. An account receivable has been created. If collected promptly, a good business relationship has probably been established. If not collected promptly, the time value of money has been lost, and a desirable business relationship has probably been compromised. If not collected at all, money and the business relationship have both been lost.

No single collection strategy will work in every situation. Some utilize internal resources, others outside agencies or lawyers. This book offers a combined strategy that first maximizes the use of existing office resources to collect the most money, and then maximizes the use of outside agencies to collect the balance at the least cost.

No magic solutions are suggested, but practical, effective techniques are offered. A computerized system of recordkeeping, accounting, and calendaring of payments is not necessary, but it does make a big difference—*in your favor.*

Chapters are included that help in the organization of an internal collection staff for the dunning effort. Sample letters and effective collection call techniques are presented. The best and cheapest skiptracing methods are covered.

Guidance is offered on when and how to best employ an outside collection agency and when to call in the lawyers. It is my hope that this book will help you take collection of accounts off the back burner and put them on the books with a positive, bottom-line impact.

Chapter One

An Overview Of Credit

Introduction

Banks are in the business of extending credit. Any business that also extends credit takes the same risk that banks take. Few businesses, however, use the same safeguards. Nevertheless, extending credit on open account to customers is an ordinary, if not necessary, part of most businesses. If managed effectively, it can contribute to profit and long-term business relationships. Managed inattentively, it will result in lost profits, financial difficulty, or ultimately, the failure of the venture.

Many small businesses rely on a trust relationship in extending credit. This is usually based on having worked with the customer before and having received payment. Past experience is important, but it is no substitute for a systematic approach to the extension of credit and collection. If credit is extended, there should be a system that monitors the status of payment, detects delinquencies and enforces payment. This system should preserve the good business relationships and terminate the hopeless losers.

Many new customers assume that credit will be extended as a part of doing business. The business owner should not make the same assumption.

Credit does not have to be extended to every prospective customer that walks in the door. Banks do not do this (at least those that have not already been taken over by the FDIC/RTC). Likewise, it is not necessary to continue credit terms for long-standing customers who do not pay as agreed.

Business credit should be earned. Immediate payment may be demanded for poor credit risks. Terms may be extended to those evaluated as good credit risks or who have proven themselves credit-worthy.

Creation of the Account

An account receivable is created when goods are furnished or services rendered without contemporaneous payment. This is an extension of credit. This type of credit is commonly referred to as an "open account." Under an open account arrangement, a customer promises to pay for goods or services on agreed-upon payment terms. After delivery and before payment on the agreed terms, the account is current. When payment is not made as agreed, the current account becomes a delinquent account.

A professional's or small business owner's cash flow is directly related to the collection of its accounts. The ability of the professional or small business owner to obtain credit is also related to the collection of her own accounts. This is true whether the professional or small business owner is on the cash or accrual method of accounting.

Most small businesses operate on the cash basis of accounting. Under the cash basis of accounting, current or delinquent accounts are not taxable as income. They are, nonetheless, assets of the business. If collected, they go on the balance sheet as cash.

Under the accrual method of accounting, current accounts are considered taxable income. Delinquent accounts are shown on the balance sheet subject to discount or explanation in the notes to the financial statements.

The Three "Cs" of Credit

Character, Collateral and *Cash Flow* have long been recognized as the standards by which credit has been extended. They remain valid for the small business owner.

The *character* of the customer may be measured by community reputation, personal experience with the customer or by the customer's reported credit history. If the prospect pays her other creditors as agreed, it is a good sign she will pay on a new open account as agreed.

Collateral will usually not be a part of an open account. Nevertheless, the invoice may provide for a security interest in the goods furnished. Many state statutes provide a lien on products or property that have been sold or serviced.

A customer's *cash flow* is the usual source of repayment. If a customer is known to be "robbing Peter to pay Paul," payment on account is likely to be a problem.

Nominal Credit

Most professionals and small business owners *do not* do a credit check, obtain a credit application, or obtain a financial statement. It is simply not practical, nor is it an accepted practice when making a regular sale or accepting a new patient, customer, or client. In these cases, two practices are important. First, professionals should obtain information that will assist in collection from the form which patients fill out when first obtaining services. (Model information forms are included in Appendix A.) Second, both professionals and small business owners should try to obtain at least a partial payment on account for each sale or service. A partial payment, made at the time of the sale or treatment, substantially enhances the prospect for payment of the balance.

Extended Credit

If more than nominal credit is to be extended, get a financial statement. Financial statements provide important information. Sample forms are found in Appendix (A). A financial statement is no substitute for a down payment. A down payment often serves as a condition to extending credit or as evidence of commitment to the relationship. The balance sheet shows short- and long-term debts. It also shows liquid assets and fixed assets. Look at the balance sheet to find out how much the owner has invested in the business.

Review the assets. Find out how much cash is on hand and how much is in banks. Real estate holdings, equipment, stock-in-trade, work-in-progress, accounts receivable, and inventory can also be yardsticks of financial health or financial disability.

Review the liabilities. Determine how much money is due within one year and how much money is owed on a long-term basis.

The profit and loss statement shows how effectively the customer's business is operating. If the prospective customer is not making a profit, payment on account is more doubtful and certainly more risky.

If a false financial statement is furnished and is relied upon when extending credit, this can provide a separate basis for recovering damages from a customer who does not pay. However, credit should not be extended on the basis of a suspected falsified financial statement. Credit obtained through fraud is a serious, sometimes criminal, matter.

Credit Reports

Credit reports on most prospective customers are usually readily available. There are three commercial credit bureaus that cover most of the country: Equifax Credit Information Services, TRW Business Credit Report, and Trans Union Credit. Information on individuals can be obtained from them for a fee.

A credit report will typically contain information about present and former residences and places of employment, outstanding loans and credit history.

Dun and Bradstreet is the best and most respected source of information on businesses. They also have some information on individuals. Dun and Bradstreet reports provide information such as: name of parent company, subsidiaries, address, officers, registered agent and address, number of employees, former names, authorized capital and par value, bankruptcies, suits, judgments, liens, UCC filings, financial information, net worth, credit limits, high and low line of credit balances, and payment history with credit providers.

Unfortunately, in order to obtain reports from any of these credit companies, it is necessary to be a regular subscriber. Subscription rates vary, and there is often a yearly contract and a minimum order requirement. It may not be worth the cost for a small business owner to be a regular subscriber.

If credit is going to be a significant part of the business relationship, sign up with a credit service. Do it *before* deciding whether and how much credit should be extended to the customer—not after the customer is indebted to you.

Credit Personnel

The person in the small business who is responsible for making the decision to permit a patient or customer to pay on account has a direct impact on bottom-line profit. Often, the owner of the small business is directly involved in the day-to-day operations. In larger companies, executive management sometimes turns this over to others. It is important that the individuals who actually have the discretion to permit a customer or patient not to pay cash receive proper training. It is also important that they be given specific operating guidelines and have their performance reviewed on a regular basis.

Credit Application

There are many credit application forms on the market today. Good forms can be found at most office supply stores or can be specially ordered from print shops. Be sure that the form you choose best fits your business needs. Sample applications are found in Appendix A.

Every business owner who extends credit has the right to demand that a credit application be completed and approved before any goods or services leave the business. Customers expect this. Do not disappoint them.

A good credit application will ask for references. It is important to check them. Incredibly, most references are not checked. Regular deadbeats know this. Credit criminals provide some of the best, though false, credit references.

New Patient Information Form

If the grantor of credit is a doctor, dentist or other medical service provider, a form is provided in Appendix A. This form should be used in conjunction with the initial patient health record form that the new patient fills out.

Chapter Two

Training Customers To Pay As Agreed

Introduction

Once a sale is made, the transaction is far from complete. Payment—the most important part—is yet to come. Prompt billing typically results in prompt payment. Customers are keenly aware of their own cost of money. Many customers are fully aware that, at some establishments, the agreed "twenty days net" means the bill can be paid in forty days. They often seek the longest free ride possible. This is why a serious approach must be taken with unpaid accounts. If not, customer abuse is invited. Many more customers will pay as agreed if they are trained to do so. This chapter will help you train your customers to pay as agreed.

Nearly Delinquent Accounts

The best account is the account that never becomes delinquent. Customers can be trained to pay on time. A small effort devoted to customer training at the beginning of the relationship can pay big dividends later and save a lot of frustration and money.

One training technique is the pre-delinquent telephone call. This works especially well on new accounts. Customer training begins when an account is five days from being due and payment has not yet been received. Contact the customer. Ask about the quality of the service, satisfaction of the product, and questions the customer may have about the transaction. Verify the customer's address. Thank the customer for the business and remind the customer that payment is due in five days. Using tact, the customer should be asked if he anticipates any problem with timely payment. If not, the training call is complete. If yes, treat the account as delinquent. Treating the account as delinquent is not unfair to the customer at this point. When the customer advises that he anticipates not being able to pay as agreed, the customer has already broken one of the promises made when the account was opened—the promise that the customer would meet the terms of payment. It is not necessary to wait for the other shoe to fall before taking protective action.

Monitor the pre-delinquent phone calls. Personnel should be adequately trained to respond to all credit policy inquiries. It is important to maintain superb customer relations. Make sure your employees understand that this is a customer service call and not a collection call. If the customer is treated like a no-good debtor before the account is fully due, you may soon see your business losing customers.

The pre-delinquent phone call method will assist you in receiving an increased number of payments on time and will give you a better idea of which accounts will not be paid on time.

Incentives

Because there are many customers who will wait to pay until the very last day that a bill is due, you may try an incentive program. For example, a plan could be developed which gives a 5% discount to customers who pay within ten days. Another type of incentive plan would earn store credit for the customer when merchandise or services are paid for at the time of order or within ten days of billing.

Chapter Three

Newly Delinquent Accounts

Introduction

Face it. Once an account is thirty days past due, it is delinquent. Even though the business relationship with the customer may be ongoing, or the professional's relationship with the patient may be fulfilling and the patient's health improving, these still do not pay the bills.

The most cost-effective way to handle newly delinquent accounts is in-house. These collections are easiest to monitor and most likely to pay. They require the least amount of effort and are the easiest to collect. This is not the time to refer them to collection agents or attorneys. Instead, collect them with your own office staff.

Your collection staff may be your bookkeeper, receptionist, secretary, office manager, or even you. Coordinate all members to the same purpose—collecting the money. The point is that this is the easiest money to collect. At least make a minimal effort to collect it.

If an in-house effort cannot be organized, skip to Chapter 9 and hire a collection agency. If you choose to turn the accounts over to a collection agency, do not wait sixty days to let the account go stale. Instead, refer the accounts for collection after forty-five days. The time value of money is important. How quickly the account is collected is often as important as how much is collected. Even though the collection agency will be getting some cream puffs, you will make more on a net basis with early referrals.

Tracking Delinquent Accounts

Accounts should be tracked as soon as they are delinquent. Whether you use a collection computer program or a manual system, accounts which have had no payments, partial payments, referral to a collection agency, or referral to an attorney should all be continually monitored.

If you choose to use a manual system, index cards and a recipe box will certainly work for businesses that have few accounts receivable collections. However, this can become cumbersome once you get a large number of accounts. It is wise to have some type of computer and software support to guide you through the collection process.

Your software should generate all the reports necessary to conduct your in-house collection. These reports include delinquent customers' names and addresses, age of accounts receivable, dollars collected and expended on a daily, weekly, monthly and overall basis.

The In-House, Three-Phase Approach

For in-house collections, my recommendation is to use a three-phase approach, such as the following:

Phase I:

1. First Phone Call—Payment is Due
2. First Letter—The Request for Payment

Phase II:

3. Second Phone Call—Payment is Required Now
4. Second Letter—The Demand for Payment

Phase III:

5. Third Phone Call—Payment is Overdue: We Will Collect What is Owed
6. Third Letter—The Threat of Further Action

The telephone is an important collection tool. Coordinate billing and dunning letters with telephone calls. Give the bill or letter enough time to get to its destination, but do not give it enough time to get lost.

Phase I

Some delinquency will result with even the best paying customers. It may be time for a little refresher training. It is important to maintain a favorable attitude toward your delinquent customers. There are many reasons why payments are not timely made. Bills are lost in the mail, forgotten, or misplaced. Businesses and individuals alike go through tough times where payment plans are necessary. But without you initiating the contact, no money is paid on the account. This is why the telephone and the demand letter are so important to the collection process: you can remind absent-minded customers and you can demand payment from seriously late customers. In all events, once the account is delinquent, it is time for prompt action.

Keep a log or file record of collection activity on each customer. This can be done manually or with a computer program. Important information to have at your fingertips includes name, current address, telephone number, person last contacted, collection effort to date, and outstanding balance. Short notes on each telephone collection contact should be made during or immediately following the conversation. Collection activity includes the dates when dunning letters were sent, when telephone contact was made, what was said, what promises were made, and the terms of any settlement. A calendar should also be kept to prompt further follow-up.

1. First Phone Call—Payment is Due

Contact accounts which are two to five days delinquent. Do not wait until the twentieth or thirtieth day. By waiting, valuable time is lost. The call on the newly delinquent account should be pleasant and professional. It should be a combination of reconnaissance (in which valuable information can be obtained) and an effort to recommit the customer to payment.

The telephone collector should follow a pattern for each collection call. The good ones do this naturally because they know it is easier and saves time. With unfamiliar customers, the collector should introduce herself as calling on behalf of the company. Address the customer as Mister or Ms. Do not use first names. This helps to maintain a formal and businesslike tone during the call. Some collectors immediately and deliberately address the customer by their first name in an effort to gain personal rapport. This can promote unnecessary degeneration and hostility. It rarely promotes payment or even the promise of payment. Explain that the call is being made because payment on the account has not been made. Attempt to gain trust and full attention. Maintain a businesslike and pleasant attitude. Show empathy where genuinely appropriate.

Inquire as to when payment will be received. If there are objections to paying immediately, identify them. Urge an immediate, partial payment. A delinquent customer's heart is located close to his pocketbook. Win his heart with a partial payment on the account. If necessary, set up a payment plan. Wrap up the conversation with a recap of each of the points concerning when and how much will be paid on the outstanding bill.

The call should determine the customer's present explanation for not paying as agreed. Misplaced bill, dissatisfaction with the product or service, and financial difficulty are common explanations. Once the customer explains the reason for nonpayment, an effective response can be made. Listen to the customer. Do not anticipate the newly delinquent customer's explanation for nonpayment. Once the customer has committed himself to an explanation, fashion the response to the customer's explanation. For example, if the customer explains that the bill has been misplaced, verify the customer's address and explain that another bill will be sent. Also explain that since payment has not been received, payment on the second bill will be expected upon receipt.

If the customer is a patient and expresses a dissatisfaction with the treatment or service rendered, reschedule a follow-up visit to determine the nature of the problem. If the patient refuses to reschedule or misses the rescheduled appointment, go to Phase II of the in-house collection process.

If the customer acknowledges difficulty in paying the balance, discuss extended payment terms in exchange for an immediate, partial payment and a commitment to meet the extended terms. Develop a credit manual with guidelines for settlements and partial payment plans which all personnel can refer to. Strive to arrange payment-in-full within three months. One payment now, followed by specific, calendared payments.

If your customers are other businesses, a poor economy and certain seasons are likely to affect timely payments. For each line of business that you service, specific payment terms will need to be developed. Stay ahead of the game by monitoring industry trends and recessions.

Calls made on newly delinquent accounts should be handled aggressively. Of all delinquent accounts, these are the ones most likely to pay. With some effort, many of your customers can be trained to be good, paying customers.

Any employee involved in the trouble-shooting and collection phases must be given adequate training. Customers can be trained to pay as agreed, and it is usually easier to train a customer than it is to collect money once the customer has become delinquent. Hands-on experience is invaluable. Help employees distinguish customers who should be handled with kid gloves and those on whom firm pressure should be applied. A list of typical situations is found in Appendix C. Along with each situation is an explanation of how to handle the problem. In addition to these form situations, develop your own list of typical or frequently encountered situations. Use your own experiences and common sense to develop an appropriate response to each situation. In this way, the company's employees will be more effective, more controlled and more businesslike than if left alone to improvise on their own in situations that can easily become adversarial. A lot of resources may have been committed to building up new business. Some investment should be made in keeping the business and training the customer to pay as agreed.

2. The First Letter—The Request for Payment

Collection letters, often referred to as "dunning" letters, are widely used in the collection industry. When used correctly, they are effective. The first dunning letter is sent shortly after the first phone call, within ten days of delinquency. It is a reminder letter. A sample Demand Letter No. 1 is shown in Appendix D.

The purpose of this letter is to confirm what was said in the phone conversation and to remind the debtor, in writing, of the promise of payment. Advantages of using dunning letters include: distribution of mass correspondence in nominal time, cost-effectiveness of production, retention of control over communication, and documentation of correspondence. The major disadvantage is the nominal effect it has on many debtor/customers. A variety of collection letters are necessary for any business's collection arsenal. Have a collection letter for each of the major situations that the business encounters. Make the procedure flexible enough so that the letters can be personalized easily. This helps to draw the attention of the customer.

Phase II

Phase I gives the customer the benefit of the doubt on his initial explanation for nonpayment. It has also provided the opportunity for extended payment terms. If the account remains delinquent or returns to a delinquent status, it is time to turn to Phase II action. Again the telephone call and dunning letter used together are more effective than either employed alone.

3. The Second Telephone Call—Payment is Required Now

Always remember to stay professional. Do not use any morality language. Do not threaten. It is important to stay focused on the issue at hand—collecting the money. Use a firm, matter-of-fact tone in your voice. The goal is to get a commitment for the money to be paid. The initial goal should be payment in full. If this is impossible, large payments over a brief period of time is the next best thing.

Always leave the conversation on a polite, but firm, note. Do not alienate the customer. The customer may be in temporary hard times and once recuperated, he may choose to use the company again if treated fairly. It is twice as hard to get money from a customer who believes he was unfairly treated. The delinquent customer should be given the impression that you plan to be reasonable, yet firm in your demands.

4. The Second Letter—The Demand for Payment

A letter sent by certified mail or overnight mail often conveys a sense of urgency to the customer. This form of delivery is more expensive than regular mail and invoices, and it takes more time to produce. However, it often pays off with results. The customer who claims the bill was never received falls quickly to certified and overnight mail, where a receipt is proof-positive of delivery.

It is advantageous to enclose a pre-addressed return envelope with the letter and invoice. It helps the customer pay the bill. It is to your discretion whether to provide the postage stamp.

The second dunning letter should point out the interest and late fees that are accruing on the account. It should remind the customer that prompt payment retains good credit and avoids the hassle and embarrassment of further collection efforts and it should give the customer a specific period of time within which to respond with payment. A sample Demand Letter No. 2 is shown in Appendix D.

Phase III

This is last chance time. It is the last chance for you to collect your money before a collection agency or an attorney takes a big cut. It is the last chance for the customer or patient to avoid professional collection activity.

5. The Third Telephone Call—Payment is Overdue: We Will Collect What is Owed

Convey the sense of urgency of the situation. This is the debtor's last opportunity to discuss this matter with you. Do not threaten illegal action. There is no reason to do so. It is counterproductive. Besides, you have the power of the law behind you and can always sue to recover the money.

Make it clear that if a timely response is not made, immediate action will result. Immediate action will mean referral to a collection agency or attorney, or that a credit reporting agency will be notified if the situation is not resolved. These professionals will not be as gracious as you have been with waiting on payments.

Do not announce actions which cannot be carried out or are not planned to be carried out. On the other hand, it is fully acceptable to advise a customer of what to expect in terms of further actions. You can tell the customer you plan on taking this to court if payment is not made. It is permissible to advise the customer of the assets that can be attached if a court issues a judgment. (See Chapter 7.)

6. The Third Letter—The Threat of Further Action

This letter confirms your conversation that the account is now being turned over to a collection agency or attorney. All future correspondence should be directed to your contact at the collection agency or your lawyer at her law firm. A sample Demand Letter No. 3 is shown in Appendix D.

Settlements and How to Sell Them

The time value of money, the internal cost of the collection effort, and the value of the ongoing business relationship weigh heavily in favor of settling disputed or nonpaying accounts. There are cost savings on both sides when a disputed or uncollected debt is settled. The business owner saves the time and expense of further collection. The customer saves his credit rating, avoids further dunning, and does not have to pay for further collection costs. Ultimately, the customer avoids wage and bank account garnishments. Make these advantages clear to the delinquent customer.

Traditionally, settlements take the form of extended payment terms or a discount for payment in cash of the undiscounted balance. Today, a settlement for bartered goods or services can provide real value. Upon reaching an agreement on settlement terms, send a written confirmation of these terms to the delinquent customer. This should always be accompanied with a request that the customer confirm his agreement by signing a copy and returning it. A sample Settlement Letter is in Appendix D.

Chapter Four

NSF Checks And Credit Card Fraud

Introduction

Nonsufficient funds ("NSF") checks are often especially difficult for businesses to collect because of the small amounts that are usually involved. Initially, these checks should be treated as delinquent accounts and escalated one level for collection activity. For example: if the check bounced after a Phase I effort, contact the customer with a Phase II approach; if the check was returned after Phase II, immediately commence a last chance Phase III effort; if the check bounced during Phase III, it's collection agency time. In other words, escalate the pressure on an NSF customer. The NSF customer gets prompt and appropriate response to his irresponsible action.

Bad checks can be minimized

Bad checks can be kept to a minimum by following a few easy steps. Your employees should be trained to follow these steps as well.

1. Review Each Check Carefully

Watch as the check writer signs. Do not accept a check that has already been signed. It could be stolen or forged. Look at the amount written numerically and in letters. Note any changes in the ink color or any areas that look suspiciously erased. Do not accept postdated checks. If a postdated check is accepted, credit is being extended. More importantly, the check writer of a postdated check may have insufficient funds.

2. Always Ask for Two Forms of Identification

A current picture identification card, such as a driver's license, and a major credit card usually will suffice. A driver's license verifies the identity of the check writer. A major credit card shows that the individual has or at least recently had good credit.

3. Have Some Type of Bad Check List in Place

There are services that list bad check writers in your area. If you do not wish to use such a service, at least keep a listing of the bad checks that have passed to you over the past year.

Some states may award the plaintiff a multiple of the amount owed (double or triple) plus attorney's fees and costs if collection must be pursued through the courts.

Credit Card Fraud

Every business, large and small, encounters fraud. Some prosecution attorneys' offices will assist in tracking down civil fraud. Most will not. Credit card fraud schemes are not uncommon. Preventive measures should be put in place to avoid such hassle, heartache, and expense. Electronic verification of each transaction, via phone line, assists in verifying credit limits and whether the credit is good.

Countless businesses are victimized on a regular basis by credit fraud criminals. These are criminals who had no intention of paying in the first place. Credit fraud is major drawback for businesses in using any type of deferred payment, whether it be for goods and services sold by credit card, check, or on account.

Chapter Five

Bankruptcy

Introduction

Bankruptcy is a part of American business. It usually signals the end of any real hope for recovery on an account. When on notice that a customer has filed bankruptcy, call the clerk of the bankruptcy court and ask for the case number and status of the filing.

Chapter 7 Liquidation

In a Chapter 7 action, the debtor (business) has gone out of business. Companies, partnerships and individuals can all file a petition under Chapter 7 of the Bankruptcy Code. The Chapter 7 debtor turns over all assets to a trustee for sale. The proceeds from the sale of these assets are distributed to the debtor's creditors after deduction of the bankruptcy trustee's fee and his attorney's fees.

Distribution of the proceeds is carried out pursuant to a schedule of priorities set out in the Bankruptcy Code. Secured creditors usually get a lawyer early in the case and are more likely to receive a distribution or at least get their collateral back. Unsecured creditors, like those with unpaid open accounts, get paid last and usually get nothing. In large Chapter 7 cases, the interests of unsecured creditors are sometimes represented by an official creditors committee. Once appointed by the Court, the official committee can hire a lawyer. This allows for effective participation in the case. The committee's lawyer is paid for by the debtor.

Under Chapter 7, individuals receive a discharge of all debts, except certain taxes and student loans. This means that all debts which were listed on the bankruptcy schedules are eliminated. Businesses do not receive a discharge of debt.

Chapter 11 Reorganization

Businesses that have some prospect for financial reorganization usually file under Chapter 11 instead of Chapter 7. Chapter 11 debtors also include individuals with complicated, extensive financial holdings or whose financial affairs are intertwined with a business venture.

Chapter 13 Adjustment of Debts of an Individual

Individuals with regular wages who wish to work with their creditors to pay off much of what is owed may choose to file under Chapter 13, rather than Chapter 7.

Under Chapter 13, a portion of an individual's wages are set aside to make monthly payments to his creditors. The payments are pro rata based on the amount owing to each creditor. The payment plan usually lasts three years.

Filing a Proof of Claim

When you learn a customer has filed for bankruptcy, do not attempt to collect any money from the customer (commonly referred to in bankruptcy as a "debtor"). The Bankruptcy Code protects the debtor from further collection activity. Persistence in collection activity after the bankruptcy filing could result in sanctions against you. The best option is to file a proof of claim with the Bankruptcy Court. A form Proof of Claim is found in Appendix B. If a substantial amount of money is owed, consult a lawyer.

First Meeting of Creditors

After you get a notice of a customer's bankruptcy, you will soon receive a notice of a meeting of creditors. This meeting is conducted by the U.S. Trustee, an official in the bankruptcy system. The purpose of the meeting is to give every creditor the opportunity to ask the debtor questions about the claims which are outstanding. It can also be used to appoint a committee of creditors or by the creditors to put the wheels in motion and have a trustee appointed in the case. The size and collateral on your claim will determine how much weight you will pull within the proceedings.

Chapter 11 and 13 Committee of Creditors

The number of individuals elected to the committee of creditors varies depending on the size of the bankruptcy. At the first committee meeting, a chairperson is elected—often the unsecured creditor who is owed the most. The chairperson arranges subsequent meetings and tries to keep them on a productive level. If you are on the committee, be prepared to attend all of the meetings. What goes on is confidential. Do not discuss the details of the meetings with the debtor unless you have the committee's permission.

Remember, as a member of the committee, you are representing all the creditors' interests, not only your own. Everyone's goal should be to collect as much money as possible for the benefit of the estate and creditors. It is important to work together. A committee that cannot agree on much cannot get much done and will end up spinning their wheels and not helping themselves. It is wise to have experts on the committee, including business lawyers, accountants and persons who understand the operations of the bankrupt debtor.

The Plan of Reorganization

The debtor-in-possession is supposed to file a plan of reorganization with the court as soon as practicable. The plan sets forth the basis that the debtor proposes to reorganize its debts and business affairs. Once the plan is approved by the court, the plan will need to be carried out and all reports should be filed as required.

Length of Bankruptcy

Depending on the size and complexity of the bankruptcy, it could last from six months to many years. The assets of the business or individual may need to be sold for cash and this may take some time. The reorganization plan may take quite a while to create and get approved.

Chapter Six

Skiptracing

Introduction

Skiptracing is the process of tracking (or tracing) the steps of a missing customer or debtor (commonly called a "skip").

When is it worth your time?

If you are following good practices for establishing an account and our three phase approach, it is worth your time to make a minimal effort to skiptrace your patient or customer. If not, and you realize the account is ninety days old, you have no information form and have not made an effort to contact the skip, then it is probably not worth your time at this point to try to trace the customer. Refer the account immediately to an agency.

Finding the Debtor

There are numerous places to look for a debtor before giving up or turning the account over to an agency. Some of these methods are listed below.

Telephone Book

The most obvious, yet overlooked method of finding someone is the phone book. Not only look for the individual or business, but look for possible relatives and ex-spouses. Giving these people a call may be the quickest way to track someone down. Ex-spouses are often particularly willing to cooperate. Also, try the operator and information to see if the person or business has moved since the phone book was printed. Sometimes a forwarding number is available.

Post Office

A practice that can be implemented immediately in both the credit and collection areas is adding a statement on each mailed envelope. That statement is: "FORWARDING AND ADDRESS CORRECTION REQUESTED." When the post office forwards the envelope to a new address, the post office will at the same time return a post card with the addressee's forwarding address. There is a nominal charge, about fifteen cents (but it may be the best fifteen cents you ever invested).

Library

The local librarian will have directories and reference manuals that will assist in the search for the skip. A wide variety of telephone books, city directories, and other useful books are available in most local libraries.

Secretary of State

The secretary of state will have information on each corporation and limited partnership registered to do business in the state. The secretary of state does not have information on individuals or general partnerships. Information that can be obtained from the secretary of state includes: current legal name of corporation, address, phone number, date of incorporation, state of incorporation, registered agent's name, registered agent's address, UCC financing statements filed against the customer, senior lienholders, and fictitious names used or being used by the customer.

County Clerk or Recorder's Office

This office, typically at the local courthouse, has information on businesses, both incorporated and not, that operate in the county. The information the county clerk or recorder can provide includes: occupational licenses, tax liens, judgments, property owned, and fictitious name listings.

Civil Court Records—Clerk's Office

Also located at the courthouse, this office can give you vital information on all lawsuits—pending and resolved—in which your customer has been involved. This office also maintains complete records on divorces, civil theft, and criminal convictions, including those for bad checks and fraud.

City Clerk's Office

This office typically has information on all city business licenses, building or environmental permits, and registrations. This could be helpful in searching to see if a company is still actively doing business in the area.

Tax Collector's Office

This office will have a listing on each car, truck, recreational vehicle, boat, and titled vehicle licensed in the county.

Department of Motor Vehicles

This office has information which can be obtained or verified over the telephone, including the customer's full name, date of birth, address at the time of issuance of the title and driver's license, social security number, and driver's license number. This is a great place to start a skiptrace.

Landlords

Check with former landlords of the skip to see if a forwarding address was left. The tenant may have left the forwarding address to get his deposit back. Often landlords have an abundance of information on the lease, such as references, bank accounts, and relatives.

City and County Directories

These reference books list the addresses of individuals and businesses. There is other valuable information in them also. Hint: try looking for the address of the property next to the last known address of the skip. Contact the neighbors. Often they know and are willing to tell about the whereabouts of the skip.

Banks

If the bank that the debtor used is known, contact that bank to determine if the account is still open and if a forwarding address has been left.

Professional Associations and Clubs

It never hurts to check with former buddies and associates. This could be at the local union hall, the Chamber of Commerce, the Rotary Club, the Jaycees, or any other club that your debtor would most likely have been a member.

Licensing Boards

If the individual is a professional who must maintain a current license to operate in the profession, call that licensing board. Most will confirm whether the license is current and may give or confirm the licensee's most currently reported address. This is the common practice for all types of physicians, lawyers, real estate brokers, and a wealth of other professions.

Former Employers

Employees often leave a forwarding address with their former employers to ensure receipt of the final paycheck. There may also be a hint as to their new whereabouts on the employment application that was filled out when they were first employed.

Credit Reporting Agencies

These are valuable skiptracing resources that should not be overlooked. Dun and Bradstreet is a commercial reporting agency. You can obtain information on a debtor company on such things as: name of parent company, subsidiaries, address, officers, registered agent and address, number of employees, former names, authorized capital and par value, bankruptcies, suits, judgments, liens, UCC filings, financial information, net worth, credit and payment history, and banking information.

Chapter Seven

Using The Legal System Without A Lawyer

Introduction

There are many cases on which you can work through the legal system yourself. Although this may sound surprising, it is true. Listed within this chapter is a guide from the beginning of the legal system to the end—the end meaning *Getting Paid in Full!*

Mechanic's Liens

One option prior to filing a lawsuit is to file a mechanic's lien. A mechanic's lien is a statutory lien available to persons who supply materials or services. The lien is an encumbrance upon property in possession of the provider of the materials or services. It secures payment of the unpaid portion of the materials or services provided. The lien can also encumber property not in possession of the provider. However, in such cases a prescribed notice must be given. This notice varies from state to state.

Some businesses that have been given this additional source of relief are: electricians, plumbers, contractors, masons, and car repair persons. Many of these businesses can file a mechanic's lien to assist in getting paid. The lien does not guarantee payment, but it does help protect your rights. A mechanic's lien is a lien placed on property and recorded at the courthouse. Before the owner of the property can sell it, all liens must be paid, including all mechanic's liens. So although the money may not come immediately, it will come when the property is sold. Most people do not want any kind of lien on their property, whether they are trying to sell it or not.

Going to Court

Because it was designed for the layman, small claims court has relaxed rules of evidence and procedure. It handles only small dollar amounts—the maximum being $500 to $5,000, depending on the state. The object of small claims court is to take the burden of strict evidentiary rules away and allow the layman to litigate his or her claim in an environment which is not as threatening as the larger civil arena. It is in the small claims arena that the average person can file a claim and get a judgment, economically, quickly, and often without an attorney's assistance.

Circuit court is designed for larger dollar cases. The rules of evidence and procedure are stricter than in small claims court. Many states require corporations to use attorneys in this arena. Even if they do not, it is often a wise idea to use one because of the large dollar amounts at risk of being lost. Often it will take more time to get a judgment because it takes longer to get a court hearing. Once a hearing date is set, discovery may be sent and depositions may be set and taken. At the hearing, there may be an opening statement, examination and cross-examination of the parties and witnesses of both sides, and closing statements.

You can count on making at least two trips to the courthouse. The first to file the claim and the second for the hearing. The claim is filed with the clerk's office.

Where to File

The claim or complaint must typically be filed in either: (1.) the county where the facts gave rise to the cause of action; or (2.) the county in which the defendant is a resident. Some states only allow the claim to be filed where the defendant is a resident.

The Clerk's Office

The courthouse can be an intimidating place for a newcomer. Do not expect any legal advice from the clerks. They are only able to give limited advice. They are not attorneys and are not allowed to practice law, but they can give you general guidance in proceeding with your case.

Some clerks' offices have specific forms used in their courts; these are the only forms which they will accept. Other clerks don't seem to mind how or on what the complaint is written.

Appendix E is a compilation of forms used in small claims court. These are only examples. It will be necessary for you to obtain the specific forms from the local clerk for the county in which you are filing suit.

Filing the Lawsuit in Small Claims Court

The document which will need to be filled out in order to initiate the proceedings is typically referred to as the Complaint, Statement of Claim, or Petition. It is the document in which you list your name or business, the defendant's name or business, the amount owed, and the reason for the debt. How detailed you need to be in stating your claim varies from courthouse to courthouse. A majority of the explanation will be done in front of the judge, so many judges require very little explanation on the Complaint itself.

There will be a fee for filing the Complaint. This amount varies also. However, it is usually a fairly reasonable sum—far less than the filing fee in circuit court.

Service of Process

After the complaint is filed, but before a claim may be brought before a judge, the defendant must be served with the complaint (See Appendix E.) Typically, once the complaint is filed with the clerk's office, the clerk will give it a case number and will stamp and/or sign the summons. It must then be served on the defendant.

There are three basic ways for serving summons. The first is service by the U.S. Mail. The second is service by a sheriff or deputy. The third is service by a private process server. Each of these three will be discussed below in greater detail. Be aware that different counties and different states allow various methods of one or more of these types of service.

U.S. Mail

Some courts allow for the service of summons through the mail, usually certified, return receipt requested. The main benefit to using this form of service is that time and expenses are saved by not serving the papers in person.

The main detriment to sending a summons through the mail is that it is not as effective in grabbing the defendant's attention. The experienced debtor will be aware of the contents of the certified letter and will refuse to sign for it at the post office. If he does not sign, it is not a valid service. At this juncture, a more expensive alternative must be chosen.

The Sheriff

Having a sheriff deliver court documents is the traditional method of impressing upon a defendant the seriousness of the matter. However, another strategy is to instruct the sheriff to serve the defendant at his place of employment. Some sheriff's offices allow this practice, others do not. It is often a highly embarrassing situation to be served a summons at work in front of colleagues. This is a strategy for you to consider.

Depending on the county, the sheriff will either serve the person and bill for his services, or he will request a fee in advance (often the actual cost of service plus mileage) before attempting service. If a defendant cannot be found by the second or third try, the sheriff often sends the summons and complaint back with a bill for the attempted service.

At this point, you may need to do a little investigation on your own to determine the location of the party and the best time and place to serve him. This can save you time with the process server.

Upon locating the party, an alias summons (see Appendix E) can be obtained from the clerk's office at a minimal charge. This summons looks just like the original summons, but has the word "Alias" typed in front of the title "Summons". Any available additional information regarding the best time and place for service can usually be noted directly on the summons.

Private Process Service

If the sheriff's office has proven ineffective, an alternative that has become quite popular over the last few years is the private process server. Private servers will often serve process for about the same cost as the sheriff's office. They are often quicker; service can be made within hours if requested. They are usually more flexible. Many will serve anywhere, anytime in order to serve your process. The clerk's office will often know of one or two reputable private process servers who are effective in the area in which the process is to be served. Inquire with the clerk of the court whether you will need a motion and an order from the judge to use a private process server. If so, there is usually a form which the clerk will furnish for use in this situation. (See Appendix E.)

Suing and Service of Process on a Business

Suing a business is much different than suing an individual. Likewise, service of process on a business is also different. The following information is useful in determining what steps to take when it is necessary to serve a summons to a business or sue a business.

Sole Proprietorships

A sole proprietorship is a business owned by an individual who is personally liable for the debts incurred by the business. Typically, the defendant is listed in the complaint and the summons first by the individual's name, followed by the name under which she is doing business. One example is: Lissa Lamoutte, doing business as ("d/b/a") L.L.'s Glamour Nails. The defendant is then served as an individual, by one of the methods described above. Once a judgment is obtained, it is enforceable to satisfy the debt against both Lissa Lamoutte and her business, L.L.'s Glamour Nails.

Partnership

There are general and limited partnerships. General partners are personally liable for debts of the general partnership. Limited partners are liable to the extent they invested in the limited partnership. When filing suit against a partnership, each general partner must be named in the complaint, followed by the term "general partner," and then followed by the name under which the partnership is doing business.

For example, A.E.R.T., a software supply company, should be listed in court pleadings as: Alan Edwards, a general partner, and Ryan Taylor, a general partner, d/b/a A.E.R.T. and Co. Once a judgment is obtained, it is enforceable against each general partner or the business. If Alan Edwards is destitute and Ryan Taylor is wealthy, it is perfectly acceptable to attempt the full amount of collection from Mr. Taylor. It does not have to be collected fifty percent from Mr. Edwards and fifty percent from Mr. Taylor.

Corporation

A corporation is treated as an entity separate from its owners or stockholders. The stockholders are not usually personally responsible for the debts of the business. In most states, a registered agent is designated by the corporation as the person to be served with legal process. Typically, this designation is made by the corporation, with the secretary of state. The correct corporation name must be listed on the court documents. This information can be obtained through the secretary of state's office.

For example, your company wants to sue Fountain's Music and More because the equipment it purchased was not paid for. Contact the secretary of state to provide the name of the registered agent who must be served in order to get effective service of process. The secretary of state may inform you that Fountain's Music and More's officially filed name is Linda Fountain's Music Headquarters for Great Tunes, Inc. It is important that on the complaint the defendant's name is written exactly as it is officially filed.

A judgment obtained against a corporation can be enforced only against the corporation and not against its employees. You may not sue the stockholders of the corporation individually. They are legally protected from personal liability by the corporate status of the company. However, there are exceptions to this rule. You may be able to obtain a judgment against the person who signed the contract or bill if he signed it individually and not as an officer of the corporation. You may also be able to "pierce the corporate veil" if the individual operates the company as his own personal business rather than a separate entity.

For example, Bob Harms, the president of the corporation TST Harms, Inc., pays his monthly home mortgage with corporate checks, buys groceries with corporate money, and buys flowers for each of his girlfriends on corporate charge accounts. In a subsequent lawsuit, it could be brought into evidence that Mr. Harms is operating the business not as a separate corporation, but as his own business. He could then be personally liable for any damages resulting from the suit.

Statute of Limitations

One fatal error is to sit on a case until the statute of limitations has run. This means that the claim was not filed within the time limits set by the state legislature. Each state has different time limits for each type of claim. It is important to check with your individual state's laws as to the time limits. The statute of limitations is tolled on the day the claim is filed with the clerk, not on the day it is heard by the court.

To compute the time remaining on your action, look to see when the wrongful act was done, or when the contract was breached. On an account where the defendant did not make a scheduled payment, the statute of limitations begins to run from time the payment was due. For example, tenant Donald Leroy moves out of an apartment before his lease term is up. The statute of limitations for filing suit against him for the rent begins to run at the time Mr. Leroy fails to pay the monthly rent that is due. From this point on, the landlord, Gail First, has only a specified period of time within which to file a complaint. This time period will vary from state to state.

Another example is Stanley, the electrician who provides electrical work to customer Ruth, who later refuses to pay for the work. Stanley the electrician has a certain period of time in which to file a complaint, starting from the date that the bill was due. Once the statute of limitations has run (i.e., the time period has expired), Ruth is home free.

However, if Ruth has made payments on the account, the statute of limitations begins to run the day the last payment was made on the account. Acceptance of partial or late payments may operate as a modification of Ruth's obligation to pay in full, on time.

The Trial

The following information is intended to assist you during that crucial period of time known as a trial. Likewise, the information is useful in showing you what you may expect during the trial process. If any of the information is unclear and you are unsure of yourself, but have not contacted an attorney, please do so.

Preliminary Hearings

The first court date is called the hearing. It is often at the hearing that plaintiff and defendant meet face to face for the first time. It is often an awkward time, especially if the parties do not have the assistance of attorneys. But it is before this hearing that the parties should get together and attempt to resolve the conflict if possible. If no compromise can be reached, go ahead and take a seat in the courtroom.

When the judge enters the courtroom, all present should rise. When once again seated, the clerk or the judge will begin calling the cases. If you are handling your own case, watch what other parties do in their cases, so that you know what to do, where to stand, when to speak. When it is your turn to be heard, approach the bench and politely respond only when asked a question. If you need more information, read *Small Claims Court Without a Lawyer,* by this same author.

Default Judgments

If you show up and the other party does not, yet was properly served, the judge will probably enter a "default judgment" in your favor. This means that the other party has defaulted its position by not appearing. The other party may petition the court within a reasonable time to get the default judgment set aside if they have a good reason. However, if the allotted time comes and goes and you have heard nothing, the judgment is deemed permanent. (Note: the timetable differs slightly from state to state.)

Be careful. Just as the judge will enter judgment in your favor if the defendant does not appear at the required time, so may she enter judgment in the defendant's favor or dismiss your case if you do not appear at the required time. If neither party appears, the judge will likely dismiss the action. Usually this dismissal is without prejudice, meaning you may refile the case with the clerk, repay the filing fee, and proceed through the steps again.

If you receive a judgment against the defendant, then a post judgment letter needs to be written to the defendant. This letter should announce that you have received a judgment and are now expecting it to be paid. It may also warn the debtor of further action you intend on taking to collect the money. (See Appendix D.)

Contested Hearings

Often, if the parties have failed to attempt to negotiate first, the judge may request the parties to step into a side room and discuss their problem. It is at this time that you need to remain calm, cool, and collected. Speak to the other party in a courteous, but "matter-of-fact" manner. Explain your viewpoint in an organized way and listen while the other party gives their viewpoint. If you are willing to negotiate, ask the other party if they are willing to settle. If they are, suggest an amount which you feel comfortable with, while still giving yourself some negotiating room. If the problem can be solved before having the court settle the matter, all parties are generally more pleased with the outcome.

If both you and the opposing party are ready to litigate the claim, the judge may do one of two things: she may hear the case that day or she may "set it over for trial" on another day. This will almost always be a bench trial, meaning the claim will be litigated in front of a judge, without a jury. It often depends on the state laws, the particular judge's style, and even how crowded the courtroom is that particular day.

If it is within the state law and the judge's style to have the case heard that very hour, you are going to have to be prepared with your witnesses and evidence. Whether the judge operates in this fashion can be discovered from either the clerk's office or the judge's secretary. If you can't find this information, it is often better to be safe than sorry. Bring your witnesses and your evidence to the first hearing.

If the judge sets the case over for trial, take advantage of the additional time. Attempt settlement negotiations, if feasible. Plan trial strategies. Go over your evidence and the testimony of your witnesses. Pick out a nice dress or suit to wear—a conservative, professional appearance never hurts.

The judge may have a variety of different ways of conducting a small claims trial. She may invite each party standing in front of the bench to speak their mind. Then she may ask a few questions and make a decision on the spot. If the issues are complex, she may ask the parties to have a seat at the respective plaintiff and defendant tables and begin hearing the case in a more formal style.

During the more formal trial, the plaintiff will first have the chance to speak, call witnesses, and introduce evidence. The defendant has the right to cross-examine each witness whom the plaintiff puts on the stand. Once the plaintiff's evidence is presented, it is the defendant's turn to speak, call witnesses, and introduce evidence. The plaintiff also has the right to cross-examine each witness that the defendant puts on the stand. Once this is complete, the plaintiff has the right to a final statement concerning the case. At this point, the judge may give her decision or take the matter under advisement and mail her decision out to the parties.

As hinted to at the beginning of this chapter, there are situations which do require an attorney's expertise—even in small claims court. This may be where the opposing side files affirmative defenses, files a counterclaim, hires their own attorney, etc. You have to weigh the odds and see what is best for your situation.

Post Judgment Proceedings

A common misconception is that once you receive a judgment, payment follows. Typically, it is far easier to get a judgment than to execute successfully on it. For example, I received a judgment against Harold's Painting Company, Inc., a Decatur, Illinois company, for splattering paint on my car while they were painting a bridge in Jacksonville, Florida. It was an easy judgment to get—they didn't show up to contest it. The judgment is now on the books at the courthouse as a valid judgment. However, I have not received the first dollar from this company. It is now up to me to pursue post judgment collection proceedings against them.

Execution on the judgment is your responsibility, not the court's. You must handle this matter in a timely fashion. The act of executing on the judgment is limited to the life of the judgment. This lifetime varies from state to state.

Execution on the judgment is typically not allowed until after a final judgment is received in a case. It may not be allowed until the judgment is recorded with the clerk's office. It also may not be allowed until after the brief time in which the defendant could file a motion for a new trial or rehearing has run.

Listed infra are the various methods used by plaintiffs in recovering monies owed. Your situation and the state you live in will determine the method best chosen for your case. Sample forms necessary are shown in Appendix E. Please note that certain clerk's offices are picky concerning the form used in their court and they may request that you use the forms provided by their office. Many a judgment isn't worth the paper it's printed on. This is why you need to know, up-front, the options that are open to you.

Garnishments for Wages, Bank Accounts, and Independent Contractors.

If the defendant is not willing to sit down and write out a check in your name, most states have provided methods of collection through garnishment. State laws vary on which funds can be garnished. For instance, the leeway given to plaintiffs with the use of wage garnishments and non-wage garnishments in Illinois is a great luxury that plaintiffs in all states do not have. For example, Florida and Texas are very debtor-oriented. It is very difficult to garnish wages, bank accounts, and real property in those states. Florida and Texas have very strict homestead exemption and head-of-household laws. Most other states fit somewhere in between these two extremes. The circuit clerk will know the rules on which collection methods are allowable in her state and county. The clerk will most likely have in her office the specific forms which the court prefers.

For example, if I wanted to collect my money from Harold's Painting Company, Inc., here in Florida, I would first need to find out if they have a Florida office. If they have property in the state of Florida, I could file a lien against that property. If they have a bank account in the state of Florida, I can garnish that account. However, if Harold's Painting Company, Inc., only has a bank account in Illinois, I will have to certify the judgment in Illinois before garnishing the account.

Wage Garnishments

The information needed for a wage garnishment is included on the Affidavit for Wage Deduction Order and a Wage Deduction Summons in Appendix E. These documents will need to be filed at the clerk's office, along with a filing fee. Some clerks prepare the documents themselves. If so, this is one less job for you. One phone call to the clerk will let you know whether you must use their forms and whether they prepare the documents. The clerk will then collect the filing fee and sign the documents. It then goes to the applicable sheriff who executes service on the debtor's employer.

Many states' instructions to an employer are similar to the following:

An employer is required to withhold the following from a non-exempt employee's salary:

> *the lesser of (1) 25% per week of the gross amount paid the employee for any work week, or (2) the amount by which disposable earnings of said employee for a week exceed thirty times the Federal Minimum Hourly Wage in effect at the time the amounts are payable.*

The term "disposable earnings" means that part of the earnings of any individual remaining after the deduction from those earnings of any amounts required by law to be withheld.

Some states allow for a continuing writ of garnishment, which allows the employer to continue garnishing the debtor's wages week after week until the debt is satisfied.

The garnishment continues in effect for a specific amount of weeks or until the debt is paid, depending on the specific state. At the completion of the stated time, the employer will send you and the court a copy of the interrogatories he has filled out. He may send the check to you directly, send it to the clerk, or may hold it and request an order from the judge to release the funds.

Different employers have different habits. Different courts have different rules. After the judgment is obtained, you can find out the habit of the particular employer by calling the payroll department of the garnished company and asking for the person in charge of wage garnishments.

If the full amount of the judgment is not garnished within the time allowed, another wage garnishment will be necessary. Retype the Affidavit for Wage Deduction Order to reflect the amount paid by the employer and the remaining amount due. Refile this with the circuit clerk's office. There may be another fee for filing. Fortunately, these fees can typically be billed to the defendant.

Non-Wage Garnishments

If you know that the debtor has a bank account with a decent sum of money in it, a non-wage garnishment is often a very quick and effective way of accessing payment for the debt. The first step is to file the necessary documents with the clerk. They will then have to be served upon the bank holding the funds. The Non-Wage Deduction Order and Summons (see Appendix E) instructs the bank to put a hold on any funds currently in the debtor's name.

For example, if I want to garnish Harold's Painting Company, Inc.'s bank account, I would wait until there is a large sum of money in the account before garnishing it. I would request the garnishment server to serve the bank the day before Harold's payday. This way, the account should have plenty of money in it. The money will then go to pay the judgment rather than Harold's employees' salaries. It is a great way to get their attention.

If your debtor is an independent contractor with money owed to him by another business, the non-wage garnishment is the avenue to use. The garnishment is served upon that business, and any monies owing the defendant are held. Monies up to the amount of the judgment are then turned over to you.

For example, Harold's Painting Company, Inc., was contracted by the state of Florida to paint a bridge. If the city still owes Harold's money for that job, I could file a garnishment on the state to hold any monies due to Harold's and pay the judgment amount first.

Depositions, Citations to Discover Assets, and Interrogatories

If you are not aware of what or where assets of the defendant may be located, a Deposition (also called a Citation to Discover Assets) is the legal avenue in which to proceed. This is accompanied by a subpoena. (See Appendix E.) The subpoena is a document requiring the debtor to appear either in court or at your place of business (depending on the state) and produce certain requested items.

For example, if I wanted to depose Harold's Painting Company, Inc., regarding the judgment I have against them, I would request that they produce their corporate officer and all books, papers, or records in their possession or control and which may contain information concerning their debt to me. If I knew of any special documents which may show where they have wealth, I would request that these are brought as well.

When deposing an individual, look for place of employment, real estate, personal property such as vehicles and boats, bank accounts, stocks and bonds, etc.

At the deposition, have the defendant fill out a questionnaire, often referred to as an Affidavit of Assets and Liabilities. (See Appendix E.) Once you are armed with this completed form, you are ready to garnish wages and bank accounts, attach property, and collect on other items the defendant may have.

Another handy tool is the credit application that the debtor may have filled out with your company. Refer to this document when discussing the matter with him. Ask questions about their banks—amount of money in the accounts, etc.

Interrogatories are another way of getting information from a debtor. This is basically the same as the deposition, but far less intimidating because the questions are written and mailed to the debtor rather than asked in-person, with a court reporter. This is a handy method when you don't have the time for additional discovery. The debtor is instructed to answer the questions within a certain number of days.

The disadvantage of this method is that it is far easier for the debtor to lie and/or "forget" that he had certain assets.

If it does not appear that the defendant has any assets, you may be stuck for the time being. However, judgments are valid for quite a few years. You are allowed by the court to repeat this deposition again in the future if you believe the circumstances have changed for the better and it is worth your time.

Rule to Show Cause (Contempt of Court)

If the debtor does not appear for the deposition or Citation to Discover Assets hearing, a Rule to Show Cause (also called a "Motion for Contempt") may be served upon the debtor. This is a document which orders the debtor to appear before the judge and explain why he was not at the deposition (Citation to Discover Assets hearing). It is often at this hearing that the judge will then order the debtor to talk with you about his assets. Upon completion, the judge may then ask both parties to step forward and inquire as to whether the debtor has been candid about his financial information and whether a payment arrangement has been agreed upon.

If the defendant-debtor does not appear for any of the hearings up to this point, depending on the state, a bench warrant may be issued for his arrest. This is often a fast way of getting a debtor's attention. Jail can have a truly sobering effect. It opens many people's eyes to the seriousness of the matter. A bond will be set by the judge, and the debtor will have to pay this bond to get out of jail. As a result of this action, you are often quickly paid. Remember, even though a debtor can't go to jail because he is poor, he can go to jail if he ignores court orders.

Attachment, Levy or Execution on Personal Property

Depending on the individual and the state, the court may allow some taking of a debtor's personal property. However, this is often a very difficult task. If you know of property owned by the debtor that is not subject to other liens and is not exempt personal property under state law, then you may request a Writ of Attachment or Execution from the clerk's office. (There may be a fee for this service.) This document is then prepared with the listing of the assets that are to be picked up by the sheriff. The writ is given to the sheriff, who will then proceed to follow its directions. A fee is paid, either to the clerk or to the sheriff, along with a bond to protect the debtor in case the assets were taken wrongfully. This is typically a substantial amount of money. By docketing the writ, you are in essence putting a lien on the debtor's nonexempt personal property in that county.

Attachment or Execution on Real Property

Once again, if you know that the debtor has real property, get a writ issued by the clerk's office. This, along with a certified copy of the judgment, needs to be filed in the county recorder's office in the county where the property is located. However, you may not be able to collect on this until the land sells because of certain exempt and homestead laws.

However, when the judgment is against a business, such as Harold's Painting Company, Inc., there are very few exemptions that protect the business. Therefore, it is often much easier to attach and execute on the property of a business.

Replevin

Replevin is an action to collect personal property which is being wrongfully held. The legal action must be brought in the county in which the property is located. Typically, the way it works is to get a writ of attachment without notice, and a bond must be posted by you, the plaintiff. The judge will issue an order. The sheriff, upon receiving all necessary paperwork, including the order and writ of attachment, will go out and take the property without any prior notice to the defendant.

Exempt Property

Each state has a list of items you cannot take from an individual, even with a valid judgment. Fortunately, these rules do not apply to corporations. Two of the more debtor-friendly states, Texas and Florida, go to great lengths to protect individuals from being wiped out should they find themselves in financial trouble. Most states give landowners some sort of exemption as a homeowner for the property on which they reside, be it a certain dollar limit which is exempt from creditors or a certain amount of acreage. For example, Florida exempts 1/2 acre in a town and 160 acres outside of town, regardless of value.

Certain states do not allow a judgment to attach to a "homesteaded" house. A "homestead" is property on which the debtor lives. In some states, even though the house is worth millions, it cannot be taken.

Heads of households have a wide scope of protection in some states. In Florida, no head of a household's wages can be attached. The legislature has said to liberally construe the situation in "the best possible light of the debtor."

Other personal property can be exempted. The dollar value of this exemption varies from state to state. Florida allows debtors $1,000 of personal property exemption. This includes furniture, cars, clothing, etc. The burden is on the debtor to prove each exemption.

Types of Property to Consider Attaching

In order to have your debt satisfied, you may want to consider attaching some of the following types of property. This list includes some of the more common items and also what information should be included on the Writ of Attachment.

Automobiles

You must be specific in the assets you are requesting. If it is an automobile, you must list, on the writ, the model, color, tag number, vehicle identification number, approximate value of the vehicle, whether it is subject to any other liens, and location of the vehicle. You can get information on a vehicle by calling the state's Department of Motor Vehicles.

Once the automobile has been seized, it will be held by the sheriff's department to be sold at a sheriff's auction. Often, the debtor will contact you before the vehicle is sold. This is a good time to negotiate with him on paying the debt. Often, if he will pay the debt and all court costs, a satisfaction of judgment can be filed, the sale can be stopped and the vehicle returned to the defendant.

Caution! Be sure that the debtor has quite a bit of equity in the vehicle. If the debtor just recently purchased the car and is paying monthly on it to a bank, that bank is going to get the first monies from the sale to pay off the debt owed them. Make sure that you are making it worth your while and your money to attach the vehicle.

Business Property

If you have received a judgment against a business, it is often possible to attach assets of the business. To establish the assets the business has and when the most money is in the cash register, you may wish to do a deposition on the company first. This way you will be fully knowledgeable and prepared when you complete the Writ of Attachment for the sheriff.

For example, if I want to attach the assets of Harold's Painting Company, Inc., for its outstanding judgment to me, I might go after their business machinery, cash register receipts, office equipment, and vehicles.

Other Personal Possessions

Furniture, boats, airplanes, jewelry, stock, and many other items may be attachable. Once again, a detailed explanation of the item is necessary for the sheriff's Writ of Attachment. If the item is a boat or an airplane, you will have to include much of the same information as is needed for an automobile. You will also need to know the approximate value of the goods, whether they are subject to any other liens, and their location.

Liens on Real Property

The threat of placing a lien on a debtor's property may well be incentive enough to persuade him to pay the judgment. A lien on real property is a legal claim to property. There can be more than one lien on any piece of property. Each will have a different priority of claim. Whether a lien is placed on a defendant's property automatically when there is judgment entered against him varies from state to state.

A copy of the judgment needs to be filed in each county in which the defendant has real property. The form, referred to as an Abstract of Judgment (or something similar), can be found at the clerk's office. Proper filing will give you a valid lien and add your name to the list of lienholders on the property.

The simple act of placing a lien on the property does not force a sale of the property. It only places a claim against the property for if and when it is sold in the future. When it is sold, the order of the liens on the property will determine in which order the profits will be divided.

Homestead laws in most states exempt part or all of a debtor's home from attachment or levy. In most states, a lien can still be put on the property, however, a creditor such as yourself may not force a sale of the property. This protection typically lasts though the life of the debtor and sometimes through the life of the spouse. The protection also lasts only as long as the debtor occupies the house and claims it to be homestead. If the debtor were to move and rent out the house, it would no longer be considered homestead and would then be leviable.

Chapter Eight

When In-House Efforts Have Been Exhausted

Introduction

You've tried collecting accounts in-house. On some it has worked; on others, it has not. But how do you evaluate the performance? Reports must be prepared and reviewed. Without accurate reports, it is impossible to evaluate performance. From evaluation, you will determine whether the in-house method is working or whether other methods need to be tested. Other methods include reporting the delinquencies to a credit bureau, employing a collection agency or employing an attorney.

Evaluating the In-House Effort

The most important question to ask in evaluating the in-house procedure is "ARE YOU MAKING MONEY?" In determining whether you are making money, consider not only the money coming in, but the money (in terms of expense) going out. If you are coming out even or losing money, the in-house collection of accounts may not be a good idea for you. If this situation does not look like it will improve, you may consider hiring outside help to work the files. With this hiring, you will get a percentage of the debt back when payment is made. This is better than breaking even or losing money.

Expenses which you will have when operating an in-house collection operation include the following:

1.) Staff—This includes the person(s) making the collection calls, sending the collection letters, handling the accounting function, handling the reporting, any secretarial support and managerial support.

2.) Phone expense—When an outside agency accepts cases, this cost is absorbed in the percentage fee they receive from the cases. However, when you are doing the work in-house, all phone bills must be paid when billed. It isn't possible to pay the phone company if and when you collect the money.

3.) Computer software and hardware—Although some small businesses are able to operate on index cards in a recipe box, most businesses have too many accounts to operate in such a way and must become computer-automated. This expense can run from many hundreds of dollars to tens of thousands of dollars.

4.) Supplies—Although many of these are small ticket items, supply costs build up quickly. Every expense spent on the collection function should be included in the equation in order to have a true view of the profits or losses of the operation.

5.) Time (as in your time)—Don't forget this expense. It is very valuable. Consider whether you are putting more hours into the collection project than it is worth.

There are probably other expenses that the author has failed to mention. Note that you would have few of these expenses if the accounts were turned over to an agency or attorney.

The way to determine whether the in-house collection process is worth the expense is to document activity on reports. Evaluate these reports. Don't expect them to look good for the first few months. You will experience a loss for a certain period of time—this is to be expected. Don't get discouraged if you don't make a lot of money at first. Review the reports weekly and monthly to see where the collections are headed. Are they headed downward, upward, or nowhere at all? The proper reports will show what age of receivables are paying the best, what type of receivables are paying the best, and which staff collectors are doing the best job.

Using Outside Agencies

We have discussed keeping the accounts in-house if it makes monetary sense. However, if such an operation cannot be put together or does not turn out to be cost-effective, it is time to look for some assistance. This is where an association, a collection agency or a law firm comes in.

It may be advantageous to file a claim with the professional organization, association, or state agency which governs that person or business. Some of these include credit bureaus like Dun and Bradstreet, Equifax, and TRW, the Chamber of Commerce, a professional association (like the bar association or medical association), the attorney general, and the state or district attorney. Each of these agencies have local and/or state offices. Most will request that the complainer fill out a special complaint form or submit a letter detailing the problem. State the facts clearly and concisely. If the agency feels that you have a legitimate grievance, they will investigate. Typically, the first step is asking for the other side's story.

Each agency has different powers to enforce complaints. Some try to negotiate with the parties to a mutually agreeable compromise. Others have strong legal powers. Some agencies, like the Better Business Bureau, don't handle this work at all. For example, the state attorney's offices can prosecute bad check writers criminally. Although it's never legal to threaten someone with filing criminal charges if they don't pay a debt, it's always proper to report delinquencies to the law and let the law take over.

If filing a claim does not work, how to refer the account to a collection agency is covered in Chapter 9, and how to refer the account to a lawyer is covered in Chapter 10.

Chapter Nine

Employing A Collection Agency

Introduction

There are many factors to consider when selecting a collection agency to represent your company in the collection of accounts receivable. Several have been listed below in order to help you select the collection agency that is best for your situation.

Local vs. Nationwide Collection Agencies

Consider whether you are looking for a local or nationwide collection agency. Many small business owners choose local agencies for convenience. Reports and files can be transferred back and forth efficiently. Face to face meetings are easy and economically feasible.

Some nationwide agencies have only one office from which all collection activity is handled. Some have regional offices. With the widespread use of 800 numbers, it is much more feasible to conduct business on a nationwide or regional basis. With today's fax machines and computer modems, distance and location are becoming less important.

Many nationwide agencies have gained the reputation of being quite professional and service-oriented. Most, if not all, will have brochures explaining services and fees and will have a sales staff to answer your questions.

Further Considerations

The type of accounts your business needs to collect will enter into the decision-making process. Are your clients consumers or businesses? Certain agencies specialize in consumer collection. Others specialize in collecting from commercial accounts. Still others specialize in collecting occupation-specific accounts such as medical or transportation accounts.

You should verify that the agency you wish to hire is licensed and bonded. Request to see the license and the bond and make sure the dates are current.

If possible, an on-site inspection should be done of the agency. If an agency does not let you into their offices, a red flag of suspicion should be raised. Check for modern techniques and equipment. To handle such a bulk of cases, any such operation should be fully computerized and efficient. Listen to the calls the collectors are making. Do they sound competent and ethical? Inspect the letters being printed. Are they professionally written? Are they overly soft or overly threatening? Are they complying with the Fair Debt Collection Practices Act? (The Fair Debt Collection Practices Act is discussed infra.)

Just as you check prospective employees' references, check agencies' references. Many agencies will be a member of the American Collectors Association—they may have recommendations. Check with the Better Business Bureau for any complaints filed. The Chamber of Commerce may be able to give you some information about the agency, such as the length of time they have been in business in the community.

Request a current client list from the agency. However, because some agencies are reluctant to make their customer list public, you may only receive a select list of references from the client list.

Get It in Writing

Ask the agency for a written agreement. Review the contract. Have your lawyer review it as well. It is so much easier to resolve matters when the agreements are in writing rather than oral.

Fee Arrangements

It is important to get a written fee schedule. Collection agencies have fee schedules which range from simple to complex. One agency may have an across-the-board fee of 1/3 of all collections. Another agency may charge a flat dollar rate for a series of letters and a percentage if the letter series does not work. Another agency may charge 1/4 for all cases collected within 30 days and 1/3 for all other cases. There are as many options for fee arrangements as there are collection agencies, so be sure to review each agreement individually.

It is also important, right from the beginning, to have a termination clause in your agreement relating to fees due to the agency. A termination clause is a portion of the agreement explaining how you and the collection agency will say goodbye at the end of the relationship. Questions to consider include: How much money is the agency going to keep if you take your cases back? Are they going to request a percentage for working the file even though the money will come in after the account is returned? It is much easier to have this laid out right from the start.

Fees charged may vary depending on several factors, the most important being age of the accounts, size of the accounts (dollar-wise), volume you will be turning over for collection, and whether the accounts have good addresses. Fees charged may also vary on the intensity of collection activity required or requested. This includes how many letters and phone calls it will take to convince the customer to pay.

Verify that the agency has a trust account for depositing money collected. Ask for a list of their procedures for handling these escrow funds.

Reports

You will want to review reports from the agency periodically. One report should show total dollars collected, dollars which are due to you, dollars which are due to the collection agency, and dollars forwarded in court costs. Another report that is handy is an activity report. Let them show you how many phone calls and dunning letters have gone out on each account. If you wish, you can even get a copy of the telephone collector's notes for each file.

Skiptracing

The most common system used to skiptrace commercial accounts is Dun and Bradstreet. The most common system used to skiptrace consumer accounts is credit bureau reports.

Both local and nationwide collection agencies will search outside of your state for lost customer/debtors. However, don't expect great results. Most agencies have a lack of incentive for finding these people, their thoughts being that if the person has skipped the state, they are unlikely to be found, and if found, they won't be threatened by an out-of-state agency demanding payment for an out-of-state debt.

Typically, there are no larger out-of-pocket expenses or higher percentages charged than those that must be paid to locate and collect money from out-of-state debtors. However, this is subject to contract negotiations.

Evaluating Performance

It is often difficult to evaluate an agency's performance. One method is to evenly divide a group of accounts and distribute them to two or more agencies. Give the agencies at least two to three months to work the files. Evaluate them primarily on amount of money collected and the time taken to collect it. Other factors to consider include the quality and timeliness of the agency's reports to you, and your general satisfaction with the professionalism of the collectors and staff. Again, remember that the main factor is: "Are they collecting the money?"

Fair Debt Collection Practices Act

Both collection agencies and collection lawyers are governed by this act. It was designed to protect individuals from certain activities that debt collectors might use to collect debts, including harassment, abuse, false or misleading representations, and unfair practices. Although individual businesses who collect their own debts are not technically included in the scope of the act, it is a good idea for each business to have a copy of this passed around the office and abided by.

Conduct which falls under the Act includes the following:

1. Using threats of harming the person, property or reputation of any person.

2. Using obscene or profane language to abuse or intimidate.

3. Publishing a list of debtors and amounts owed in anything but a credit bureau report.

4. Constant telephone badgering.

5. Contacting a debtor at unreasonably early or late hours, or at unreasonable times at work.

6. Not disclosing the caller's identity.

7. Misrepresenting that the caller is an attorney or is affiliated with the government.

8. Stating that a crime has been committed when it is a civil dispute and/or stating that the debtor could be arrested.

9. Sending misleading documents which appear to have come from the court or from an attorney.

10. Giving or threatening to give false or misleading credit information to others.

11. Threatening any legal action which is unlawful.

12. Threatening any legal action which the collector does not intend to take.

13. Collecting an amount greater than the debt, unless the law allows.

14. Depositing postdated checks early.

15. Making collect phone calls.

16. Sending collection notices on postcards.

17. Putting the collection agency's name on the envelope mailed to the debtor.

Validation of Debts

The collection agency must, in its initial contact or within five days thereof, send the debtor a written statement explaining how much is owed and to whom. Also included is a statement that the debt will be assumed to be valid unless the agency hears from the debtor within thirty days. If the debtor does so notify the agency, the agency must provide verification of the debt to the debtor. Also within the thirty day period, the debtor may request that the agency provide the original creditor's name and address, if different from the current creditor.

Disputed Debts

If the debtor notifies the debt collector within thirty days that he disputes the bill, all collection of that bill must stop until the debt collector can provide verification of the bill to the debtor.

Multiple Debts

Where a debtor owes money on two or more accounts handled by the same debt collector and mails in a payment specifying which bill to apply the payment to, payment must be applied to that account. The debt collector cannot choose which account the debt is to be applied.

Where Legal Action May Be Brought

The bill may be litigated in one of two locations: either the county where the debt was incurred, or the county where the debtor currently resides.

Damages

Debt collectors who fail to comply with the Fair Debt Collection Practices Act can be liable for:

1. The actual amount of damage sustained by the debtor.
2. Up to $1,000 in additional damages.
3. Court costs and attorney's fees.

Factors that go into deciding the amount of damages include the frequency of noncompliance with the Act and the nature and extent to which the noncompliance was intentional.

Note that if the debtor brought the action for purposes of bad faith or harassment, the tables can be turned and the debtor may be liable for the attorney fees of the debt collector. As a precautionary measure, ask your collection agency whether they have ever been sued for violation of the Act and if so, the circumstances behind the case(s).

Dispute Resolution with the Agency

There are three usual ways to resolve a dispute with your collection agency: negotiation, arbitration, and litigation. Unless your contract provides for arbitration, you will have the two usual alternatives of negotiation and litigation. In a negotiation, you will find that you often have the weaker position. The agency has the money and you don't. Litigation, on the other hand, is often not cost-justified for either party. This usually results in an impasse, which tends to benefit the agency.

Arbitration, an alternate dispute resolution technique, is usually more cost-effective and satisfactory than either of the two alternatives. In arbitration, an independent, neutral party acts to persuade both sides to accept a fair compromise of the dispute. Ideally, lawyers are not involved on behalf of either party, although the involvement of lawyers does not preclude an effective arbitration. It usually just makes it more expensive. You will not be able to compel your collection agency to arbitrate a dispute unless you have provided for arbitration in the contract with the agency.

The Federal Trade Commission is the federal agency charged with monitoring collection agencies. They may be able to give you some assistance, but don't rely on it. Collection agencies are also regulated by state authorities. In Florida, for example, it is the Florida Department of Insurance. Again, unless the agency has committed a crime or engaged in a fraudulent practice, state government agencies do not usually provide meaningful assistance in a customer's relationship with the agency. They are far more likely to be interested in protecting the rights of the people the agency is trying to collect the money from than protecting the rights of the businesses the collection agency is trying to collect the money for.

Discharging the Agency

There are a number of reasons you may wish to terminate your relationship with a collection agency: unsatisfactory performance, untimely or inaccurate reporting or accounting for money collected, and unprofessional conduct. The best way to terminate this relationship is with a face-to-face conversation with the agency's representative, followed by written notice pursuant to the contract with the agency. This is another important provision of your contract with the agency. You should have the right to terminate the agency with or without cause, at your discretion, with written notice. Ten to thirty days is a common notice period.

On termination, the agency will usually retain certain rights. For example, the agency will retain its right to claim a share of money received on accounts that had been referred prior to the time that the notice of termination became effective. This right would include the right to receive money from accounts that have previously been worked by the agency, but were not actively being worked, as well as money received on active accounts.

Chapter Ten

Calling In The Lawyers

Introduction

There are two good reasons to call in the (right) lawyers: (1) when the amount owed is large enough to have an impact on your company's financial condition if it is not collected timely, and (2) as a last resort to in-house and collection agency efforts. Many lawyers will profess to be interested in collecting your accounts. Few can do it cost-effectively.

Most professionals and small business owners have an established relationship with an attorney. The attorney engaged for the most recent real estate closing or divorce and the lawyer who is your current neighbor are not usually good choices. Sometimes it can be an expensive and frustrating experience. A good business or commercial lawyer is well-suited to help with the final and most difficult phase of collection. If you have an established relationship with a business or commercial lawyer, contact her first about handling the final phase of collecting your accounts. If you do not have an ongoing relationship with a business or collection attorney, consider making one or look for a collection attorney.

A collection attorney focuses her practice on representing creditors (like business owners, professionals, and financial institutions) in collecting money which is owed. A collection lawyer is not usually a fully-experienced commercial lawyer, real estate lawyer, divorce lawyer, or malpractice defense lawyer. She collects money from people who owe it. Collection lawyers often have separate listings in the yellow pages of the telephone book. Look there first. Call at least two and ask for an initial consultation. If she is unwilling to provide an initial consultation for free, go on to the next one listed. Remember, you are not hiring a personal attorney or a general legal advisor, and you are not looking for a friend. You are hiring a lawyer to collect your money from people who owe it and have refused to pay it.

Try to set up the interview at your place of business so that she can review, firsthand, your own in-house collection efforts, results, and records. Try to avoid having the initial interview at the collection attorney's office. This is not critical, but it is helpful in your selection process. Most good collection attorneys will want to come to you to see for themselves the status of the accounts to be collected. Most others are going to prove to be too busy, too inattentive, too ineffective, too expensive, or too lazy. There will be exceptions in both cases.

Do not carry the selection process too far. As a practical matter, finding a decent lawyer to take on accounts you have already worked using this system will not be easy. The task will be less difficult by showing an organized collection system rather than one in disarray.

Collection Attorney Fees

Collection attorneys work under three forms of payment: hourly rate, flat fee, and contingent fee. The hourly and flat fee arrangements can work to your advantage in some, but not most cases. Usually, the best arrangement is the contingent fee arrangement.

Hourly Fee Arrangement

If you are hiring the attorney on an hourly basis, you will be billed each time you make a call to the attorney to ask a question. All time spent on the case will be charged to you regardless of the result. This arrangement works best in cases involving a large amount of money and where the business owner or professional can afford the resources (usually monetary) needed.

Flat Fee Arrangement

This is usually the worst of both worlds for the client and the lawyer. The client fixes the cost of the representation, but provides little incentive for the lawyer to produce a result in terms of money collected. Many attorneys are reluctant to use this method.

The Contingent Fee Arrangement

Under this arrangement, the attorney will be advanced his out-of-pocket expenses, like filing and service fees. Upon collection of money, the attorney will be entitled to between 25-50% of the actual recovery. A one-third (1/3) contingency fee is usually the standard. If the accounts have been effectively worked in-house or by a collection agency or are more than 180–270 days past due, expect to end up at the upper end of the range. If the accounts have not been heavily worked in-house or by an agency and are less than 180–270 days past due, negotiate for a contingent fee percentage between 25% and 33%. An established collection lawyer will usually be able to evaluate your accounts and to provide a proposal to collect them. At some point, haggling over a percentage point or two can become counterproductive to establishing a good working relationship with this professional.

The attorney, when sending her bill, will often send along a description of the charges. If you have a question concerning the billing, it is acceptable to ask it. Ask what certain descriptions mean and how work in the future can be provided more effectively.

You, as a client, have an obligation to your attorney. You have a duty to be candid about the accounts that are to be collected, their age, how they have been worked, and whether they are subject to any known defenses. Be complete in your description of the age of the accounts, prior collection efforts, and possible defenses to the legal collection effort. If the account has not paid after in-house or collection agency efforts, most likely there is a problem. Either the customer cannot pay, or there is, in the customer's mind, some real complaint about the service rendered on the product purchased. The collection attorney knows these characteristics. The defense of malpractice or product liability claims is rarely covered by the fee arrangement with a collection attorney.

Be prompt for appointments made in the attorney's office or at your office. Bring papers which are important to the case. Be organized. Just as you wish to be paid on time, pay your attorney promptly. A client who pays on time is more apt to get prompt service in return.

Chapter Eleven

Preventing And Minimizing Problems With Collecting Your Accounts

Introduction

Here are some steps that can save you time and money in the management of your accounts receivable:

1. Collect when the sale is made and service is rendered.
2. Bill promptly.
3. Document the sale.
4. Make a point of contacting nearly delinquent accounts.
5. Follow up on delinquent accounts with the three step pattern of: letter, phone call; letter, phone call; letter, phone call.
6. If in business, use written contracts rather than oral.

The following paragraphs offer some quick tips using written documents that can help you in the collection process.

Written Contracts

Wherever possible, a written contract for goods sold on credit should be obtained. Written contracts eliminate many disputes. Also, having witnesses sign the contract and getting the signatures notarized help even more. The notarization proves that the other party has signed the paper. Having witnesses sign proves that the they were present when the deal was made, and their memories can help clear up points of dispute.

The contract should also contain these items: the name of the parties, a description of the product or the service to be provided, the amount of payment, payment terms and interest, late fees, and collection charges. Wherever possible, get personal guarantees. Officers of the corporation can bind a corporation; however, if the corporation goes out of business and there is no personal guarantee, the provider is typically left with no recourse.

Oral Contracts

Oral or verbal promises are often legally binding, but are often more difficult to enforce. This is because they are so hard to prove. Often, it is one person's word against another's. Avoid this situation whenever possible.

Promissory Note

A promissory note is a writing in which your customer promises to pay you the specific amount of money that is due. Be sure to include the date the money is due. Include an interest rate if the money is not paid on time and a statement allowing for your court costs and attorney fees if you are forced to take legal action to collect the debt. (See Appendix A.)

Letter of Credit

A letter of credit is a negotiable instrument designed to extend credit or pay money to the benefit of someone on the credit of another. It is almost always issued by a bank and typically used in overseas transactions.

Co-signer

A co-signer is another person who agrees to pay the purchase price for the goods or services if the original customer cannot or will not pay. Having a co-signer also works as leverage against the original customer. Most people would feel guilty if their friends or relatives end up on the hook for something for which they are responsible. If the customer is married, have both husband and wife sign. Both will be held liable. Most states have laws that prevent creditors from taking assets owned jointly by a husband and wife, unless both have signed the agreement.

Guarantee

A written guarantee is a promise of one person to pay if another does not. It is similar to a co-signer arrangement. A guarantee is very beneficial in many instances. For example, if a minor is requesting goods or services, a parent may be asked to guarantee that payment will be made as promised.

Know Your Customer

Always have a customer or patient complete a credit application. At a minimum, if payment is not made, it will assist in location of the delinquent customer. Does this person have a good job? Does she have other property that makes her a good credit risk? The more information you have about a person or business, the better suited you are to protect yourself from unforeseen problems.

Deposits/Security

Landlords and equipment rental firms have the age-old problem of collecting the rent on time. This is one reason a security deposit is typically demanded up-front. As with other businesses who extend credit, a credit application should be completed and references checked before rental.

Final Note

Stay organized. Keep all of the old invoices, bills, and other records of the transaction. The best method in the collection process is to be prepared with the paperwork. Have ready all documents which relate to the account to be collected. Almost any judge is inclined to give more weight to written evidence than to oral claims.

Chapter Twelve

Tax Consequences Of Bad Debt

Introduction

Bad debt can harm or destroy a business. However, some of the burden may be shared with the Internal Revenue Service. There are several requirements you must meet in order to be entitled to claim a tax deduction for bad debts.

What Constitutes Bad Debt?

A bad debt is treated differently, depending on whether it is incurred in a personal or business transaction. Whether it is a business or personal debt almost always depends on the purpose for which the money was used at the time it was borrowed. If the debt is personal, it cannot be deducted until it is wholly worthless, and it can only be deducted as a limited capital loss and not as a business loss. If it is a business debt, it must still pass rigid tests to be deductible. A business cannot deduct a bad debt unless it actually lost cash on the account, or unless the business has previously reported income from the sale of the item. Debts owed on account of unpaid services are generally not deducted.

Tax Consequences Of Bad Debt

Few businesses give out cash, and only businesses using the accrual method of accounting report income from a sale for which no payment is received.

A manufacturer using the cash method of accounting can deduct all costs of production as they are incurred. Since the cost of the product has already been deducted, if the sale price is not paid, it cannot be deducted.

By contrast, businesses using the accrual method of accounting report income when a sale is made, even if it is not paid for. When the account is not paid, these businesses can deduct the unrecovered sale price because it had been previously reported as income.

When qualified, a bad debt can be deducted in part or in whole whenever it becomes a "bad" or uncollectible debt. The taxpayer has the burden of proving when the debt becomes uncollectible. This can be proved from events such as bankruptcy, insolvency, closing the business, death, or nonpayment after diligent collection efforts. Consult your tax advisor before trying to deduct your unpaid accounts from your taxable income. The IRS is very touchy about this area.

Conclusion

Conclusion

This book has covered all the main areas of managing delinquent accounts receivable. If you need further information on following through with legal action on your own, my book, *Small Claims Court Without a Lawyer,* will help.

Sample letters, forms, and documents are attached in the Appendixes. Remember that these are general forms. They can be changed for your particular situation.

I hope that this book has been of assistance to you and that you end up *Getting Paid in Full!*

Appendix A

Sample Credit Applications, Information Sheets, And Notes

Credit Application for an Individual

Your Company
Company Address

The undersigned requests [your company] to extend credit on the basis of this application.

____
Name

____
Street Address

____
City State Zip Code

____
Length at current address

____
Prior address if less than two years at above address

Bank Information

____
Checking Account Name of Bank and Address Account No.

____
Savings Account Name of Bank and Address Account No.

Outstanding Obligations

____
Bank Loans

____
Mortgages

____
Credit Cards

The information furnished above is accurate and complete. I hereby give my permission to [your company] to complete a credit check on myself and check my references. The undersigned promises to pay for all goods/services obtained by the undersigned from [your company].

_______________________ _______________________
Applicant Date

I understand that the following payment terms will apply should I be approved by (your company):

1. payment within _____ days
2. all payments shall be made by (cash, Visa, Mastercard, money orders, personal check, company check)
3. all payments shall be guaranteed by (name of third party)

Credit Application for a Business

Your Company
Company Address

The undersigned requests [your company] to extend credit on the basis of this application.

___
Business Name (including any d/b/a, a/k/a, f/k/a, etc.

___
Street Address

___
City State Zip Code

___
Prior address if less that two years at current

___
Nature of business

___
Type of business (sole prop., ptnrshp, corp.)

___
Length of time in business Number of employees

___
___
___
___
___
___
Owner, Partners, or Officers names and addresses

___
Name of Accounts Payable employee for our contact

Bank Information

___
Checking Account Name of Bank and Address Account No.

Outstanding Obligations

___
Bank Loans

___
Mortgages

Credit Application For A Business (page 2)

References within the Trade

Please list below three references of businesses you purchase from on a regular basis.

____

Name of Reference   Address   Phone No.

____

Name of Reference   Address   Phone No.

____

Name of Reference   Address   Phone No.

I hereby give my permission to ___(your company)___ to complete a credit check on the above listed business and check its references.

____

Authorized Applicant and Title   Date

I understand that the following payment terms will apply should I be approved by _(your company)_:

1. payment within ____ days
2. all payments shall be made by (cash, Visa, Mastercard, money orders, personal check, company check)
3. all payments shall be guaranteed by (local bank, credit union, third party, etc.)

Note: The applicant cannot transfer or assign his/her/its rights under this application to any other party without _(your company)'s_ written approval.

Patient Credit Information

Name

Street Address

City State Zip Code

Length at current address

Prior address if less that two years

Occupation

Employer and Business Address

Social Security Number

Spouse's Name

Spouse's Employer and Business Address

Spouse's Social Security Number

Do You Have Insurance? If So, Name of Insurance Company

Name and Address of Nearest Relative Not Living With You

Please read the statement below and if acceptable, sign and date on the line provided.

I, the undersigned, agree to pay for all services rendered by this office and will pay for such services at the time they are performed. If this is impossible, I will speak with one of the members of the doctor's staff to make arrangements for payment. If payment is not made as agreed, this office may take all legal action necessary to collect the money owed. Further, I agree to pay for all action necessary to collect this money, including collection fees, filing and service fees, attorney's fees and postjudgment fees.

Patient Date

Witness

Note

$__________________ ____________________, 199_

For Value Received, the undersigned jointly and severally promise to pay to the order of the principal sum of ________________ dollars ($______) payable as follows: __________________ dollars ($_______) on the first day of each and every month. Interest shall be at the rate of 18%, per annum, payable on the whole amount of said principal sum remaining from time to time unpaid. Principal and interest are payable in lawful money of the United States of America, or such other place as the legal holder hereof may from time to time in writing appoint.

Presentment, notice of dishonor, and protest are hereby waived by all makers, sureties, guarantors and endorsers hereof. This note shall be the joint and several obligation of all makers, sureties, guarantors and endorsers, and shall be binding upon them and their successors and assigns.

Any notice to Borrower provided for in this Note shall be given by mailing such notice by first class mail addressed to Borrower at the Property Address stated in the corresponding credit application, or to such other address as Borrower may designate by notice to the Note holder. Any notice to the Note holder shall be given by mailing such notice by first class mail, return receipt requested, to the Note holder at the address stated in the first paragraph in this Note or at such other address as may have been designated by notice to Borrower.

There shall be no penalty for prepayment. There shall be a late charge equal to 5% of the amount due for all payments not received within five days of the due date.

IT IS HEREBY EXPRESSLY UNDERSTOOD AND AGREED, that, if default be made in the payment of any of the said installments of principal or interest, aforesaid, and any portion thereof shall remain due and unpaid for a period of thirty days after the same shall have become due and payable as aforesaid, the principal sum above mentioned, or any balance that may appear to be unpaid thereon, together with all arrearages thereon, shall, at the option of the legal holder hereof, thereupon become immediately due and payable, without notice, and shall be collectible immediately or at any time after such default, anything hereinbefore contained to the contrary notwithstanding. This note shall bear interest at the highest rate allowable by law if said note is in default. If suit is brought to collect this Note, the Note holder shall be entitled to collect all reasonable costs and expenses of suit, including but not limited to, reasonable attorney's fees.

Dated this _______ day of ____________________, 199_.

____________________	____________________
Witness	Borrower
____________________	____________________
Witness	Guarantor

Personal Financial Statement

Section 1 - Individual/Application Information	Sec. 2 - Other Party/Co-Applicant Information
Name	Name
Residence Address	Residence Address
City State Zip Code	City State Zip Code
Position or Occupation	Position or Occupation
Business Name	Business Name
Business Address	Business Address
City State Zip Code	City State Zip Code
Years with Business	Years with Business
Res. Phone Bus. Phone	Res. Phone Bus. Phone

Statement of Financial Condition as of ______________________, 199____

Section 3 Balance Sheet (attach additional schedules as needed)

Assets	**Dollars**	**Jt***	**Liabilities**	**Dollars**	**Jt***
Cash and Short-term Investments (Schedule A)			Outstanding Credit Card Balances		
Stocks & Bonds (readily marketable) (Schedule B)			Taxes Payable		
Unlisted Securities (Schedule C)			Policy Loan (life insurance) (Schedule D)		
Notes Receivable & Accounts Receivable			Mortgages & Obligations Due (Schedules F & G)		
Cash Surrender Value-Life Insurance (Schedule D)			Notes & Accounts Payable (Schedule H)		
General/Ltd Partnership Interests (Schedule E)			Other Liabilities (list):		
Retirement Accounts					
Personal Accounts					
Personal Property					
Automobiles					
Real Estate-Personal Residences (Schedule F)					
Real Estate-Investments (Schedule G)					
Real Estate Investments(Direct & Partnership Interests)(Schedule I)**					
Other Assets (list):					
TOTAL ASSETS			TOTAL LIABILITIES		
			NET WORTH (total assets minus total liabilities)		

Personal Financial Statement (cont'd)

Section 4 - Income Statement

Annual Income	Applicant	Co-Applicant	Annual Expenses	Applicant	Co-Applicant
Salary			Home Mortgages (Principal & Interest)		
Bonus and Commissions			Loan Payments (including other R/E)		
Interest and Dividends			Income Tax (State & Federal)		
Alimony, Separate Maintenance, Child Support***			Planned or Required Investments/ Partnership Contributions		
Capital Gains			General Living Expenses		
Real Estate Income			Other Expenses (list):		
Other Income (list):					
GROSS INCOME	$	$	TOTAL EXPENSES	$	$

Section 5 - Contingent Liabilities (including brief description)

	Applicant	Co-Applicant
As endorser or guarantor on notes/leases/contracts:		
On letters of credit:		
Current or pending suits or other litigation:		
Other (Partnership, etc.) explain:		
TOTAL	$	$

*Please check if jointly held.

**Schedule I should be used by individuals with extensive real estate investments where additional data may be needed or required by the Bank to properly evaluate the borrower's financial condition. It can be used instead of Schedule G. Because it will not be completed by most borrowers or guarantors, it is a separate schedule not printed on this Personal Financial Statement. If it is appropriate for you and has not been provided, please request it from the Bank.

***Alimony, separate maintenance, and/or child support income need not be revealed if you do not wish to have it considered as a basis for repaying this obligation.

Schedule A: Cash & Short-term Investments (certificates of deposit, commercial paper, money market funds, etc.)

Name of Institution	Savings Accts ($ amount)	Checking Accts ($ amount)	Other Short-term Investments (type and $ amount)	Total	Pledged? Y/N	Owners Code

Schedule B: Stocks and Bonds (include U.S. Government and Marketable Securities)

Number of Shares or Face Value (Bonds)	Description	Market Value	Margin? Y/N	Restricted? Y/N	Pledged? Y/N	Owners Code*

Personal Financial Statement (cont'd)

Schedule C: Unlisted Securities

Number of Shares	Description	Source of Value	Value	% of Company Owned	Pledged? Y/N	Owners Code*

Schedule D: Life Insurance Carried (include individual and group insurance)

Name of Insurance Company	Owner of Policy	Beneficiary	Face Value	Policy Loans	Cash Surrender Value	Assigned? Y/N

Schedule E: General and/or Limited Partnership Interests (Please attach K-1)

Name of Partnership	Type of Investment	Limited / General	Amount Invested	Fair Market Value of Interest	Annual Contribution Required	Pledged? Y/N	Owner Code*

*Owners Code: A=Applicant AC=Joint Account of Applicant and Co-Applicant JC=Joint Account of Co-Applicant and another party C=Co-Applicant

Schedule F: Real Estate (personal residences)

Description/Address of Property	Mortgage Holder	Maturity Date	Title in Name of	Purchase Date	Cost	Present Loan Balance	Monthly Payment	Market Value

Schedule G: Real Estate Investments

Description /Address of property	Mortgage Holder	Maturity Date	% Owned	Title in Name of	Purchase Date	Cost	Present Loan Value	Market Value	Total Annual Rental Income	Monthly Loan Payment	Other Expenses

Schedule H: Notes & Accounts Payable (also include credit lines and other commitments even if unused)

Name of Creditor	Orig. Amt. of Loan	Payment/ Repayment Terms	Maturity Date	Interest Rate	Description of Collateral (if any)	Balance Owing	Debtors Code*

*Debtors Code: A=Applicant AC=Joint Account of Applicant and Co-Applicant JC=Joint Account of Co-Applicant and another party C=Co-Applicant

Personal Financial Statement (cont'd)

Personal Information

Do you have a will?
__ Yes __ No If yes, name of executor:

Number of Dependents _____
Age __________________

Are you a partner or officer in any venture other than described on schedules?
__ Yes __ No If yes, describe:

Are any assets pledged other than as described on schedules?
__ Yes __ No If yes, describe:

Have you ever been declared bankrupt?
__ Yes __ No If yes, describe:

Are there any outstanding judgments against you?
__ Yes __ No

Do you have disability insurance?
__ Yes __ No

Income tax settled through (date)

Alimony, Child Support/Maintenance Expense $

The information contained in this statement is provided for the purpose of obtaining, or maintaining credit with (company) on behalf of the undersigned or person, firms or corporations in whose behalf the undersigned may either severally or jointly with others, execute a guaranty in (company's) favor. Each undersigned understands that (company) is relying on the information provided herein (including the designation made as to ownership of property) in deciding to grant or continue credit. Each undersigned represents and warrants that the information provided is true and complete and that (company) may consider this statement as continuing to be true and correct until a written notice of a change is given to (company) by the undersigned. (Company) is authorized to make all inquiries it deems necessary to verify the accuracy of the statements made herein, and to determine the credit worthiness of the undersigned. (Company) is authorized to answer questions about its credit experience with the undersigned.

Date Signed	Signature (individual)	Social Security #	Date of Birth
Date Signed	Signature (other party)	Social Security #	Date of Birth

Appendix B

Sample Proof Of Claim Form

Proof Of Claim

United States Bankruptcy Court
_________DISTRICT OF ___________________

PROOF OF CLAIM
Judge:________________
Chapter:_______________

____
Name of Debtor

____
Bankruptcy Case No.

A. CREDITOR INFORMATION

(The creditor is the person or other entity to whom the debtor owes money or property)

Name and Address of Creditor

____

____

____

____

______ Check here if you never received any notices from the bankruptcy court in this case.

______ Check here if this address differs from the address on the envelopes sent to you by the court.

______ Check here and attach copy of assignment if claim has been assigned to you.

Number by which creditor identifies debtor:

____

Check here if this claim:
____ replaces
____ amends a previously filed claim dated: _____________________
____ supplements

B. CLAIM INFORMATION

1. BASIS FOR CLAIM:
   ____ Goods purchased
   ____ Services performed
   ____ Monies loaned
   ____ Other forms of contract (identify)
   ____ Personal injury/Wrongful death/Property damage
   ____ Other (Describe briefly): ______________________________________
   ____ Wages, Salaries and Commissions (Fill out below)
   ____ Unpaid services performed from ______________ to _______________
   ____ Nature of services (Describe briefly): ___________________________
   Your social security number: ___________________________________

2. DATE DEBT WAS INCURRED: _____________________________________

3. **CLASSIFICATION OF CLAIM:** Under the Bankruptcy Code all claims are classified as one or more of the following: (1) Unsecured non-priority, (2) Priority, (3) Secured. It is possible for a claim to be a party in one category and partly in another - such as wage claim which may be a priority claim for the first $2,000 and an unsecured non-priority claim for the balance. Classify the nature of the claim by CHECKING THE APPROPRIATE BOX OR BOXES which you believe best describes the claim. STATE THE AMOUNT OF THE CLAIM.

   UNSECURED NONPRIORITY CLAIM $ ____________
   For the purpose of this form, a claim is unsecured if there is no collateral, or to the extent the value of collateral is less than the amount of the debt.

   SECURED CLAIM $ ____________
   Attach evidence of perfection of security.
   Brief description of Collateral
   ____ Real Estate ____ Motor Vehicle ____ Other ____________________

   PRIORITY CLAIM $
   Specify the priority of the claim by checking the appropriate box(es).
   ____ Wages, salaries or commissions (up to $2000, earned not more than 90 days before filing of the bankruptcy petition or cessation of the debtor's business whichever is earlier) - 11 U.S.C. §507(a)(3)
   ____ Contributions to an employee benefit plan - 11 U.S.C. ß107(a)(4)
   ____ Up to $900 of deposits toward purchase, lease, or rental of property or services for personal, family or household use - 11 U.S.C. ß507(a)(6)
   ____ Taxes or penalties of government units - 11 U.S.C. ß507(a)(7)
   ____ Other specify: ____________________

4. **TOTAL AMOUNT OF CLAIM:**
   $ ________ + $ ________ + $ ________ = $ ________
   (Unsecured) (Secured) (Priority) (Total)

5. Attach copies of documents in support of this claim such as purchase orders, invoices, itemized statements of running accounts, contracts, court judgments or evidence of security interests if the documents are not available, explain. If the documents are voluminous, attach a summary.

6. This form should not be used to make a claim for expenses incurred after the filing of the bankruptcy petition. Such expenses may be paid only upon proper application and notice pursuant to 11 U.S.C. ß503.

7. **CREDITS AND SETOFFS:** Attach an itemization of all amounts and dates of payments which have been credited against the debt. Set forth any setoff or counterclaim which the debtor may have against your claim.

8. To receive an acknowledgment of the receipt of your claim, enclose a stamped, self-addressed envelope and a copy of your claim.

C. CERTIFICATION

The undersigned certifies under penalty of perjury that the debtor named above is indebted to the claimant in the amount shown, that there is no security for the debt other than that stated above or in an attachment to this form, that no unmatured interest is included, and that the undersigned to make this claim.

____
Date, Sign and Print the Name and Title if any of the Creditor or Other Person Authorized to File this Claim (attach copy of power of attorney)

Penalty for Presenting Fraudulent Claim: Fine of up to $500,000 or imprisonment for up to 5 years, or both. Title 18 U.S.C. ß152 & 3623.

Appendix C

Sample Scripts

When Working With Individuals

Example One

Customer's reason for nonpayment:

"I'm a little short this month and can't afford to pay."

Appropriate Response:

"How much of the payment can you send today?" *Wait for reply.* "When do you get your next paycheck?" *Wait for reply.* "Then I can expect to see the remaining portion at that time?" Once the answers are given, specify the dates when payment must be mailed and received by. Make notes of this information for follow up.

Example Two

Customer's reason for nonpayment:

"I was not happy with the service/product and do not intend to pay."

Appropriate Response:

"May I ask the reason for your dissatisfaction?" *Find out why the customer is claiming to be unhappy and attempt to resolve the complaint if it is legitimate. If the customer expresses only partial dissatisfaction, request partial payment. Reserve resolution of the dispute and the balance of the payment for a future date.*

Example Three

Customer's reason for nonpayment:

"I was laid off from my job."

Appropriate Response:

"I am sorry to hear that. These are difficult times for many of our customers. That is why the company has given me the authority to set up a payment plan."

Example Four

Customer's reason for nonpayment:

"I never received a bill."

Appropriate Response:

"In that case, we need to verify your address. Could I have the street, city, and zip code please?" *If the wrong address has been used, let the customer know that a duplicate bill will be mailed immediately and the expected payment terms. If the correct address was used, the customer is probably using this as an excuse to stall or avoid payments. Advise that customer that another bill will be sent by certified mail which the customer will have to sign for. This will eliminate that the customer's excuse and communicates a serious attitude about payment. These customers are best given only a short period of time (ten days) to pay the second bill.*

Example Five

Customer's reason for nonpayment:

"My spouse was supposed to pay that bill according to our divorce settlement."

Appropriate Response:

"The divorce settlement is between you and your spouse. We did not sign it. We are not bound by it. Because you signed the agreement with our company for the goods/services, you are liable to us for the amount billed. You will need to see your lawyer about collecting money from your spouse."

Example Six

Customer's reason for nonpayment:

"I sent that payment last week."

Appropriate Response:

"Can I have the check number and date you sent it? We'll watch for it for the next couple of days. However, if it does not arrive, we will need you to issue another check immediately."

When Working With Businesses:

Example One

Customer's reason for nonpayment:

"We ran into a financial problem this month and can't afford to pay."

Appropriate Response:

"How much of the payment can you send today?" *Wait for reply.* "When does the company get its next payment from its customers?" *Wait for reply.* "Can I expect to see the remaining portion at that time?" *Once the answers are given, specify the dates on which payments are to be made. Always make timely delivery of payment the customer's responsibility.*

Example Two

Customer's reason for nonpayment:

"The company was not happy with the service/product and does not intend to pay."

Appropriate Response:

"We are always concerned when someone is not fully satisfied with our service/product. What seems to be the problem?" *Wait for reply.* "Our service manager will be in contact with you shortly to try to work this out."

Example Three

Customer's reason for nonpayment:

"We've had some tough economic times."

Appropriate Response:

"Yes, I understand. This recession has put a squeeze on many pocket-books. We understand this and are willing to work with you. We can divide the bill into two payments. The first payment will be due this month on the 15th. The second will be due on the 15th of next month."

Example Four

Customer's reason for nonpayment:

"The company has never received the bill."

Appropriate Response:

"In that case, we need to verify your address. Could I have the street, city, and zip code please?" *If the wrong address has been used, let the customer know that a duplicate billing will be mailed immediately and the expected payment terms.*

If the correct address was used, the customer is probably using this as an excuse to stall or avoid payments. Advise the customer that another bill will be sent by certified mail for which the customer will have to sign. This will verify that the customer received the bill. It also communicates a serious attitude about payment. These customers are best given only a short period of time (ten days) to pay the second bill.

Example Five

Customer's reason for nonpayment:

"We have had a large turnover in our accounts payable department and have not gotten to all the bills."

Appropriate Response:

"I'm sorry to hear that things are confused at this time. But, it is very important that this bill is paid within the next five days in order to keep your good credit rating with our company. Is there anything I can do from my end to assist you?"

Appendix D

Sample Letters

Credit Information Requested Letter

(Date)

(Debtor)
(Street Address)
(City, State Zip Code)

Re: Account #

Dear (Ms./Mr. Debtor),

Thank you for your order. We are currently processing your request and would like to complete the order as promptly as possible. In order to accomplish this, we will need either a check in the amount of $ ________________ or a completed and approved credit application.

Once again, thank you for your order and we look forward to receiving the above request.

Sincerely,

(Mr./Ms. Businessperson)

Employment Information Requested Letter

(Date)

(Debtor)
(Street Address)
(City, State Zip Code)

Re: (Customer's Name)

Dear (Sir/Madam),

Your above named employee has requested credit from our company. Please confirm the employment. We shall keep such information in confidence. Your employee has authorized this request.

To confirm this employment, please complete the questionnaire below and return it to us at your earliest convenience.

Sincerely,

(Mr./Ms. Businessperson)

(Employer) is authorized to supply the following information to (Your Company) for the purpose of being granted credit.

____
Employee's Signature

____
Employee Number and Department

Position held: ________________

Salary: ____________________

Length of Employment: __________

____
Employer's Signature

Pre-delinquent letter

(Date)

(Debtor)
(Street Address)
(City, State Zip Code)

Re: Account #

Dear (Ms./Mr. Debtor),

Thank you for doing business with our office. We are appreciative of your business. If you have any questions about the attached invoice (or the invoice recently received), please contact our office. As indicated on the invoice, payment should be received in our offices no later than (date) to keep your fine credit rating with our company. You are a valued customer and we look forward to serving you in the future.

Sincerely,

(Mr./Ms. Businessperson)

Newly Delinquent Letter/First Letter—The Request for Payment

(Date)

(Debtor)
(Street Address)
(City, State Zip Code)

Re: Account #

Dear (Ms./Mr. Debtor),

Thank you for doing business with our office. We are appreciative of your business and would hope to continue our excellent business relationship. Our records show that you are __#__ days late in paying on your account. We know that this is probably an oversight and that you intend to forward the balance immediately. Please consider this to be a friendly reminder.

Sincerely,

(Mr./Ms. Businessperson)

Second Letter—The Demand for Payment

(Date)

(Debtor)
(Street Address)
(City, State Zip Code)

Re: Account #

Dear (Ms./Mr. Debtor),

As of today's date we have not received the payment due on your account. If payment is not made immediately, your credit privileges with our company will be suspended.

Please contact us to make arrangements for payment.

Sincerely,

(Mr./Ms. Businessperson)

Third Letter—The Threat of Further Action

(Date)

(Debtor)
(Street Address)
(City, State Zip Code)

Re: (Account #)

Dear (Debtor),

Your immediate attention in paying the debt owed in the amount of $______ for(merchandise/services) is necessary to avoid further action being taken against you.

If you do not make payment in full by (______), a lawsuit will be filed against you. A hearing date will be set and you will be notified by summons at (your residence or place of employment). If you do not pay the amount due prior to the hearing date and do not appear for the hearing, a default judgment will be entered against you. A recorded judgment will be a lien against your property and will be a record on your credit report. If you do appear for the purpose of contesting the bill, a trial date will be set.

(The following is optional.)

It is our policy not to accept installment payments on the debt. However, in some cases exceptions are made. I am enclosing an affidavit which you may complete and return to me. You may make an offer of installment payments in the space provided near the bottom of the page. This statement will not be accepted unless it is signed under oath before a notary public.

Please let me know your intentions as to this matter by (date).

Sincerely,

(Accounts Receivable Department)

Payment Plan Letter

(Date)

(Debtor)
(Street Address)
(City, State Zip Code)

Re: Account #

Dear (Ms./Mr. Debtor),

Thank you for your offer to pay ($____) per (week/month) on the above account. As agreed, I am willing to accept ($____) payments per month for (_#_) months until this debt is satisfied. The payments are due on the (___) of each (week/month), beginning (day, month and year) and continuing (weekly/monthly) through (day, month and year.)

As agreed, as long as the payments are made in a timely fashion, we will withhold all further action.

Thank you for your cooperation in this matter.

Sincerely,

(Accounts Receivable Department)

Delinquent Payment Plan—Letter A

(Date)

(Debtor)
(Street Address)
(City, State Zip Code)

Re: (Account #)

Dear (Debtor),

It is apparent that you have not fulfilled our agreement to make payments on the above referenced account. The agreement was to pay ($______) per (week/month). Please remit the delinquent balance of ($_____) immediately. Mark the remaining dates on your calendar in order to avoid missing these agreed upon dates in the future.

Thank you for your immediate cooperation in this matter.

Sincerely,

(Accounts Receivable Department)

Delinquent Payment Plan Letter—B

(Date)

(Debtor)
(Street Address)
(City, State Zip Code)

Re: (Account #)

Dear (Debtor),

On (____date____), we agreed to a (monthly/weekly) payment arrangement of ($__________). Although the first payment was made on (_date_), we have not received the following payments. We are anxious to work with you in this matter to bring you up to date on your obligation. Please contact the office immediately or send in the delinquent balance.

If we do not hear from you in the next (_____) days, we will be forced to collect this debt through legal avenues. We look forward to hearing from you and clearing up the delinquent balance.

For your convenience, enclosed please find a return envelope for your convenience.

Sincerely,

(Accounts Receivable Department)

Settlement Letter

(Date)

(Debtor)
(Street Address)
(City, State Zip Code)

Re: (Account #)

Dear (Debtor),

As orally agreed, my company is willing to accept ($________) as a full and complete settlement of your account.

This sum must be paid by (date) or this offer will become void.

Thank you. We look forward to receiving this payment.

Sincerely,

(Accounts Receivable Department)

Post Judgment Letter

(Date)

(Debtor)
(Street Address)
(City, State Zip Code)

Re: (Account #)

Dear (Debtor),

Unless I receive your immediate cooperation in making a payment arrangement on the judgment which has been entered against you, I will have no alternative but to proceed with further legal action. This may include a deposition to determine your assets and liabilities. You will be forced to produce all records requested and appear at a designated time and place for this examination. Other alternatives include garnishments, both of wages and bank accounts.

If you wish to avoid further legal action, please contact me at once at the above number by (_date_). Thank you for your attention to this matter.

Sincerely,

(Accounts Receivable Department)

Appendix E

Sample Legal Forms

Small Claims Complaint—General

STATE OF ___________
IN THE CIRCUIT COURT OF THE ______ JUDICIAL CIRCUIT
COUNTY OF ___________

____
Plaintiff

Case No. _______________

v.

____
Defendant

COMPLAINT

NOW COMES the plaintiff, _________________ and complains of the defendant, _____________________, and states as follows:

1. That plaintiff is an individual/partnership/corporation, residing at: ____.

2. That the defendant resides at ________________________________.

3. That the defendant has failed to pay $ ________ to plaintiff for expenses incurred while (___________________).

4. These expenses include ($ ____________ for _____________). (See Exhibit A.)

5. That the total amount owing is $ ____________ and plaintiff has requested and defendant has failed to make payment of this amount.

WHEREFORE, plaintiff, ________________ , respectfully prays that judgment be entered against defendant, ______________ , for the sum of $ _________ , plus court costs.

By____
Plaintiff

Plaintiff _________________________ City _____________________

Address _________________________ Phone ___________________

Small Claims Complaint—Automobile

STATE OF ______________
IN THE CIRCUIT COURT OF THE __________ JUDICIAL CIRCUIT
COUNTY OF ___________

____
Plaintiff

Case No. __________________

v.

____
Defendant

COMPLAINT

NOW COMES the plaintiff, _______________ and complains of the defendant, ________________, and states as follows:

On or about __________ in the vicinity of _________________ on a public highway of ___________ County, ___________, plaintiff's motor vehicle, being operated by ____________________ was in a collision with defendant's motor vehicle being operated by ________________ with defendant's consent, and that said collision with plaintiff's vehicle was caused by the negligent and careless operation of defendant's vehicle, whereby plaintiff's vehicle was damaged and depreciated in value.

WHEREFORE plaintiff demands judgment in the sum of $ _________.

____
Plaintiff

Plaintiff ______________________ City ___________________

Address ______________________ Phone _________________

Small Claims Complaint—To Evict Tenant

STATE OF _______________
IN THE CIRCUIT COURT OF THE ___________ JUDICIAL CIRCUIT
COUNTY OF _____________

____
Plaintiff

Case No. _________________________

v.

____
Defendant

COMPLAINT

NOW COMES the plaintiff, ________________ and complains of the defendant, ___________________, and states as follows:

1. This is an action to evict a tenant from real property in __________________ County, __________________.

2. Plaintiff ______________ is the agent for the owner of the following described real property in ______________ County, _______________:

3. Defendant ______________ has possession of said property under oral/written agreement to pay rent of $_______, payable ___________.

4. Defendant _______________ failed to pay rent due ______________.

5. Plaintiff _____________ served Defendant _________________ with notice on _________________ to pay said rent or deliver possession but Defendant _________________ refused to do either.

WHEREFORE Plaintiff ________________ demands judgment for possession of said property against Defendant.

____
Plaintiff

Plaintiff _________________________ City _____________________

Address _________________________ Phone ____________________

Small Claims Complaint—On An Account

STATE OF ________________
IN THE CIRCUIT COURT OF THE ___________ JUDICIAL CIRCUIT
COUNTY OF _____________

____
Plaintiff

Case No. ___________________________

v.

____
Defendant

COMPLAINT

NOW COMES the plaintiff, _________________ and complains of the defendant, ________________, and states as follows:

1. This is an action for damages which does not exceed the sum of $ (small claims limit) , exclusive of interest and costs.

2. There is now due, owing and unpaid from the Defendant to the Plaintiff monies in the sum of $ _________ since __________ , 19___ for:

(check one)

______ Goods sold and delivered by Plaintiff to Defendant according to the attached itemized statement and/or account.

______ Work done and materials furnished by Plaintiff to Defendant at Defendant's request, according to the attached itemized statement and/or account.

______ Services rendered by Plaintiff to Defendant at Defendant's request, according to the attached itemized statement and/or account.

_____ Monies due from Defendant to Plaintiff according to the attached account.

WHEREFORE Plaintiff demands judgment in the sum of $_______ plus court costs.

____
Plaintiff

Plaintiff __________________________ City ______________________

Address __________________________ Phone ____________________

Small Claims Complaint—Replevin

STATE OF ______________
IN THE CIRCUIT COURT OF THE ___________ JUDICIAL CIRCUIT
COUNTY OF ____________

____
Plaintiff

Case No. ____________________

v.

____
Defendant

COMPLAINT

NOW COMES the plaintiff, _______________________ and complains of the defendant, ______________________, and states as follows:

1. That plaintiff is/are lawfully entitled to the possession of the following described personal property, located at __________________________ ___________________ in ____________ County, ____________, to wit:
______________________(description of property)______________________
____

2. Defendant came into possession of the above said goods by virtue of ______
____
____

3. To the best of my knowledge, information and belief the value of said property is the sum of $___________, that said property has not been taken for any tax, assessment or fine levied by virtue of any law of the state of ___________, nor seized under any execution or attachment against the goods and chattels of said plaintiff liable to execution and that the above named defendant has/have possession of the above described personal property and wrongfully detains the same from plaintiff in the County of _______________, State of ______________________.

4. That said plaintiff is the owner of said personal property and entitled to the possession thereof by virtue of ____ ________________that said defendant ________________, in ____________ County, ______________, wrongfully detains from said plaintiff said personal property of the value as aforesaid; that said plaintiff made demand upon said defendant for possession of said personal property prior to the institution of this claim, yet said defendant continues to wrongfully withhold possession thereof from said plaintiff _______________, for the reason being __________ ____.

5. Said plaintiff demands the return of said personal property and damages for the wrongful detention thereof or for the value thereof and the costs of this action.

____
Plaintiff

Plaintiff ____________________________ City ______________________
Address ____________________________ Phone ______________________

Summons by Certified Mail

STATE OF ________________
IN THE CIRCUIT COURT OF THE ____________ JUDICIAL CIRCUIT
COUNTY OF ______________

____
Plaintiff

Case No. ____________________________

v.

____
Defendant

SUMMONS BY CERTIFIED MAIL

To each defendant:

YOU ARE SUMMONED and required to appear before this court at ________ ____________________ at ___ o'clock, __.m., on __________, 19 ___, to answer the complaint in this case, a copy of which is hereto attached. IF YOU FAIL TO DO SO, A JUDGMENT BY DEFAULT MAY BE TAKEN AGAINST YOU FOR THE RELIEF ASKED IN THE COMPLAINT.

(seal of court) Witness ______________________, 19_____

____
(Clerk of the Court)

____

_________________, on oath says the last known mailing address of defendant _________________, is ____.

Signed and sworn to before me ____ ______________________, 19____

____
(Notary Public/Clerk of Court)

____

Plaintiff ____________________________ City ________________________

Address ____________________________ Phone ______________________

CERTIFICATE OF MAILING

A copy of this summons was mailed to each defendant named in the above affidavit, addressed to each at the address shown, by certified mail, return receipt requested, on ______________, 19____.

_______________________________ By ______________________________
(Clerk of Court) (Deputy)

(Seal of Court)

Summons

STATE OF ________________
IN THE CIRCUIT COURT OF THE ____________ JUDICIAL CIRCUIT
COUNTY OF ______________

____
Plaintiff

Case No. ______________________

v.

____
Defendant

SUMMONS

To each defendant:

YOU ARE SUMMONED and required to appear before this court at ____ ________________________, at ___ o'clock, __.m., on __________, 19___, to answer the complaint in this case, a copy of which is hereto attached. IF YOU FAIL TO DO SO, A JUDGMENT BY DEFAULT MAY BE TAKEN AGAINST YOU FOR THE RELIEF ASKED IN THE COMPLAINT.

To the officer:

This summons must be returned by the officer or other person to whom it was given for service, with indorsement of service and fees, if any, immediately after service and not less than 3 days before the day for appearance. If service cannot be made, this summons shall be returned so indorsed.

This summons may not be served later than 3 days before the day for appearance.

(seal of court) Witness __________________, 19______

____
(Clerk of the Court)

____

Plaintiff _________________________ City ____________________

Address _________________________ Phone ____________________

Alias Summons

STATE OF ________________
IN THE CIRCUIT COURT OF THE ____________ JUDICIAL CIRCUIT
COUNTY OF ______________

____
Plaintiff

Case No. ______________________

v.

____
Defendant

ALIAS SUMMONS

To each defendant:

YOU ARE SUMMONED and required to appear before this court at ____ ________________________, at ___ o'clock, __.m., on __________, 19___, to answer the complaint in this case, a copy of which is hereto attached. IF YOU FAIL TO DO SO, A JUDGMENT BY DEFAULT MAY BE TAKEN AGAINST YOU FOR THE RELIEF ASKED IN THE COMPLAINT.

To the officer:

This summons must be returned by the officer or other person to whom it was given for service, with indorsement of service and fees, if any, immediately after service and not less than 3 days before the day for appearance. If service cannot be made, this summons shall be returned so indorsed.

This summons may not be served later than 3 days before the day for appearance.

(seal of court) Witness ________________, 19_____

____
(Clerk of the Court)

____

Plaintiff __________________________ City _____________________

Address __________________________ Phone ___________________

Motion For Private Process Service

STATE OF ________________
IN THE CIRCUIT COURT OF THE __________ JUDICIAL CIRCUIT
COUNTY OF ______________

MOTION FOR LEAVE TO USE PRIVATE PROCESS

COMES NOW the Plaintiff, ______________________ and moves the Court pursuant to state law for leave to serve the Defendant(s) in this cause by private process through ________________________, and states as grounds therefore the following:

(1) Plaintiff retains __________________________ as its private process server throughout the state of __________________, which substantially reduces the cost of this action and, ultimately, the cost to Defendant(s) upon judgment;

(2) Service of process will not prejudice the rights of Defendant(s) in any manner;

(3) Private process will be in the best interests of justice and will relieve additional burden of this court.

____
Plaintiff

Plaintiff ______________________

Address ______________________

City __________________________

Telephone _____________________

Order For Private Process Service

STATE OF ____________________

IN THE CIRCUIT COURT OF THE ____________ JUDICIAL CIRCUIT

COUNTY OF __________________

ORDER GRANTING LEAVE TO USE PRIVATE PROCESS

UPON Plaintiff's motion, and the Court being otherwise fully advised;

Now therefore, it is hereby ORDERED that Plaintiff be granted leave to serve the Defendant(s) by private process through __________________, an employee of ______________________.

Entered:_____________________________

____

Judge

Plaintiff _____________________________

Address ____________________________

City _________________________________

Telephone ___________________________

Entry Of Appearance, Stipulation For Judgment

STATE OF ____________________
IN THE CIRCUIT COURT OF THE ____________ JUDICIAL CIRCUIT
COUNTY OF __________________

(You, d/b/a
Your Business)

PLAINTIFF

V.

CASE NO. _________________________

(John D. Debtor)

DEFENDANT

ENTRY OF APPEARANCE, STIPULATION FOR JUDGMENT

Plaintiff and Defendant each enter their appearance herein, waive service of process, and stipulate that this Court enter judgment against Defendant for Plaintiff in the amount of $____________ plus the cost of this suit.

____
Plaintiff

____
Defendant

Subscribed and Sworn to before me

_________________________, 199___.

____
Notary Public

Affidavit For Wage Deduction Order

STATE OF ____________________
IN THE CIRCUIT COURT OF THE ____________ JUDICIAL CIRCUIT
COUNTY OF _________________

(___________________________)
PLAINTIFF

V.

CASE NO. _________________

(___________________________)
DEFENDANT

AFFIDAVIT FOR WAGE DEDUCTION ORDER

___________________ on oath states:

1. Judgment was entered in this case on ___________, 19___, in favor of judgment creditor __________________ and against judgment debtor for $___________ and costs.
2. $_________ has been paid on the judgment.
3. There is unpaid on the judgment:
   - $_________ principal
   - $_________ costs
   - $_________ interest
   - $_________ TOTAL
4. I believe employer _________________ is or will be indebted to the judgment debtor for wages due or to become due.
5. The lasts known address of the judgment debtor is: _____________

____

I request that summons be issued and directed to the employer.
Signed and sworn to before me

____
Plaintiff

____________________,19____.

____
Notary Public

____

Plaintiff __________________________
Address __________________________
City ______________________________
Telephone _________________________

Wage Deduction Summons

STATE OF ____________________
IN THE CIRCUIT COURT OF THE ____________ JUDICIAL CIRCUIT
COUNTY OF ________________

(________________________)
PLAINTIFF

V.

CASE NO. ______________________

(________________________)
DEFENDANT

WAGE DEDUCTION SUMMONS

TO THE EMPLOYER:

YOU ARE SUMMONED and required to file answers to the judgment creditor's interrogatories, in the Office of the Clerk of this Court at the Courthouse, ________(City)__________, ___(State)___, on or before _____________, 19___. However, if this summons is served on you less than 56 days before that date, you must file answers to the interrogatories on or before a new return date, to be set by the court, not less than 56 days after you were served with this summons.

You must not file your answers to the interrogatories sooner than 56 days after service of this summons. This proceeding applies to non-exempt wages due at the time you were served with this summons and to wages which become due until the expiration of your payroll period ending immediately prior to 56 days after you were served with this summons.

IF YOU FAIL TO ANSWER, A CONDITIONAL JUDGMENT BY DEFAULT MAY BE TAKEN AGAINST YOU FOR THE AMOUNT OF THE JUDGMENT UNPAID.

To the officer:

This summons must be returned by the officer or other person to whom to was given for service, with indorsement of service and fees, if any, immediately after service. If service cannot be made, this summons shall be returned so indorsed. This summons may not be served later than the above date.

WITNESS __________________, 19____

____
(Clerk of the Court)

(Seal of Court)

By: ________________________________
(Deputy)

Plaintiff ______________________________________
Address ______________________________________
City ____
Phone ____

Affidavit For Garnishment—Non-Wage

STATE OF ____________________
IN THE CIRCUIT COURT OF THE ____________ JUDICIAL CIRCUIT
COUNTY OF _________________

(__________________________)
PLAINTIFF

V.

CASE NO. ______________________

(__________________________)
DEFENDANT

AFFIDAVIT FOR GARNISHMENT- NON-WAGE

______________________________ on oath states:

1. Judgment was entered in this case on ____________, 19___, in favor of judgment creditor __________________ and against judgment debtor for $__________ and costs.

2. $__________ has been paid on the judgment.

3. There is unpaid on the judgment:

$__________ principal
$__________ costs
$__________ interest
$__________ TOTAL

4. I believe garnishee __________________ is indebted to the judgment debtor or has in his possession, custody or control property belonging to him or in which he has an interest.

I request that summons be issued and directed to the garnishee.

____
Plaintiff

Signed and sworn to before me

____________________,19____.

____
Notary Public

Plaintiff ________________________________
Address ________________________________
City ___________________________________
Telephone ______________________________

Garnishment Summons—Non-Wage

STATE OF ____________________
IN THE CIRCUIT COURT OF THE ____________ JUDICIAL CIRCUIT
COUNTY OF _________________

(__________________________)
PLAINTIFF

V.

CASE NO. _____________________

(__________________________)
DEFENDANT

WAGE DEDUCTION SUMMONS

TO THE EMPLOYER:

YOU ARE SUMMONED and required to file answers to the judgment creditor's interrogatories, in the Office of the Clerk of this Court at the Courthouse, ________(City)________, ____(State)____, on or before ______________________, 19____. However, if this summons is served on you less than 10 days before that date, you must file answers to the interrogatories on or before 14 days after that date.

IF YOU FAIL TO DO SO, A CONDITIONAL JUDGMENT BY DEFAULT MAY BE TAKEN AGAINST YOU FOR THE AMOUNT OF THE JUDGMENT UNPAID.

To the officer:

This summons must be returned by the officer or other person to whom to was given for service, with indorsement of service and fees, if any, immediately after service. If service cannot be made, this summons shall be returned so indorsed. This summons may not be served later than the above date.

WITNESS _____________________, 19______

____
(Clerk of the Court)

(Seal of Court)

By: ____________________________________
(Deputy)

Plaintiff ______________________________
Address ______________________________
City _________________________________
Phone ________________________________

Subpoena

STATE OF ______________________
IN THE CIRCUIT COURT OF THE ________________ JUDICIAL CIRCUIT
COUNTY OF ____________________

(_________________________)
PLAINTIFF

V.

CASE NO. _______________________

(_________________________)
DEFENDANT

SUBPOENA

TO: ____________________

YOU ARE COMMANDED to appear before the Circuit Court at __________
_______________________________________on _____________, 19____
at _____ ___m. to be examined under oath concerning the property or income of, or indebtedness due _________________________. Judgment was entered on _______________, 19_____. $______________ remains unsatisfied.

YOU ARE COMMANDED to produce at the examination:

and all books, papers or records in your possession or control which may contain information concerning the property or income of, or indebtedness due judgment debtor.

YOU ARE PROHIBITED from making or allowing any transfer or other disposition of, or interfering with, any property not exempt from execution or garnishment belonging to the judgment debtor or to which he may be entitled or which may be acquired by or become due to him, until the further order of court or termination of the proceedings. You are not required to withhold the payment of any money beyond double the amount of the judgment.

YOUR FAILURE TO COMPLY WITH THIS CITATION MAY SUBJECT YOU TO PUNISHMENT FOR CONTEMPT OF THIS COURT OR TO A JUDGMENT FOR THE AMOUNT UNPAID.

WITNESS, _______________________,19___
(CLERK OF THE COURT)

NAME ________________________________
ADDRESS _____________________________
CITY ________________________________
TELEPHONE ___________________________

(Seal of Court)

DATE OF SERVICE ______________________

Affidavit of Assets and Liabilities

I, ______________________________, defendant in this case, on oath state the following:

Name ______________________________ Date of Birth ________________
Address ___________________________________ Phone ________________
City ______________________________________ State _________________
Place of Employment ____
Length of Employment ___________ Occupation _____________________
Spouse's name ____
Spouse's Place of Employment _____________________________________
Length of Employment ___________ Occupation _____________________
Earnings:

____________ per month from employment

____________ per month from pension, trusts, welfare, workman's compensation, retirement, disability, or any state, federal, local or private benefit plan.

____________ per month from other sources

Assets:
Home or other dwelling $_________________________
Address: ____
Car $_________________ Make ____________________________ Year _____
Checking Acct. $_____________ Bank ________________________________
Savings Acct. $ ______________ Bank ________________________________
Other Assets _________________________

____

I offer to pay $_______ per month, beginning ________________, 199___.

I certify the forgoing is true to the best of my knowledge and belief.

____
(signature)

Subscribed and Sworn to before me

______________, 199___.

____
Notary Public

Appendix F

Rules To Live By

Never

NEVER threaten action you are not willing or able to carry out.

NEVER be less than businesslike to a customer.

NEVER wait more than ten days to begin collection work on a newly delinquent account.

NEVER become angry, rude or sarcastic with a customer over an overdue bill.

NEVER let anyone other than the debtor or spouse know the purpose of the collection call (without permission of the debtor).

NEVER contact a debtor who is represented by an attorney without permission of the debtor.

NEVER continue collection efforts against a bankrupt individual or company.

NEVER use first names.

Always

ALWAYS get written contracts or notes when dealing with credit.

ALWAYS get credit reports run on customers before giving credit.

ALWAYS identify yourself and your company at the beginning of a collection call.

ALWAYS be courteous and businesslike when dealing with the delinquent customer.

ALWAYS try for payment in full.

ALWAYS strive to have the customer make a commitment to pay, preferably in writing.

ALWAYS offer the debtor alternatives.

ALWAYS turn down unrealistic arrangements.

ALWAYS insist that the debtor write down the payment terms.

ALWAYS record your work.

ALWAYS ask details of promised payment.

ALWAYS verify employment of the debtor and his spouse.

ALWAYS follow up with promises of payment within two days of nonpayment.

ALWAYS exhaust all sources of money for possible payment.

ALWAYS appeal to honor and pride.

ALWAYS get agreements in writing with outside agencies which will do the collection work.

Glossary

AFFIRMATIVE DEFENSE—Any new matter which constitutes a defense. Defense must be raised in the answer to the complaint or it cannot be raised.

APPEAL—The act of taking your claim, once a judgment is made at the lower court, to the next higher court for another determination.

ATTACHMENT—The act of having the sheriff collect goods owned by a person who owes you money from a judgment.

BANKRUPTCY—An all too common practice in the 1990s. The act of wiping away your debts. An individual may go through this process every seven years. A bankruptcy will stay on credit reports for approximately ten years.

CITATION TO DISCOVER ASSETS—A court hearing after you have received a judgment where the debtor is required to answer your questions as to his assets and liabilities and how he plans on paying the judgment off.

COMPLAINT—The first document filed with the court in a small claims proceeding. This document will typically list the plaintiff and defendant, the reason the plaintiff is suing, and the dollar amount.

CONTEMPT—A proceeding or an order from the judge saying that an individual has not followed the judge's orders. A criminal charge that may have serious consequences, i.e. jail.

CONTINUANCE—The judge may grant additional time to either party so that they have more time to prepare their case.

CO-SIGNER—The individual who signs a contract obligating himself to the contract. Often used when primary signer has inadequate credit or is a minor.

CREDITOR—Synonymous with plaintiff. The individual who is owed money by another.

DAMAGES—The dollar amount you are claiming.

DEBTOR—Synonymous with defendant. The individual who owes money to someone else.

DEFENDANT—The individual who is being sued.

DEMAND LETTER—A letter sent by a creditor to the debtor requesting payment on the debt.

DEPOSITION IN AID OF EXECUTION—A proceeding after a judgment is received. An investigation of the debtor under oath to determine a debtor's assets and liabilities.

DISPOSABLE INCOME—Net income, amount of income after taxes, and court ordered deductions, such as alimony, are taken out.

DISTRESS OF RENT—When a landlord sues to get the amount of rent owed to him, but he is not trying to evict the tenant.

EXTENSION—The judge may grant additional time to either party so that they have more time to prepare their case.

FILING FEE—The amount you have to pay the court in order to start the proceedings. You must pay the fee when you file the lawsuit.

FILING SUIT—The act of filing the complaint and summons with the court clerk, getting a case number, and quite probably, a court date.

FORCIBLE ENTRY AND DETAINER—The procedure by which a landlord evicts a tenant from his property and obtains a judgment for back rent and/or property damage.

GARNISHMENT—The act of taking the debtor's property toward satisfaction of the judgment, whether it be wages, bank accounts, stock, bonds, etc.

HEARING—The first time you will meet the judge. At this meeting, both sides will tell their side of the story. Depending on the court, the judge will either make his determination at this time or set a new date for a formal trial.

HOMESTEAD EXEMPTION—Most states protect homeowners to some extent from judgments and creditors. Some or all of their property may be exempt from most court actions.

INJURY—How you have been wronged. What it is that has been broken and needs fixed. See also "damages."

JUDGMENT—An order given by the judge declaring that one party has won the case.

JUDGMENT LIEN—A document which is either automatically or manually filed with the clerk stating that a person is indebted to you for a certain amount of money.

JURISDICTION—Whether the court has the power or ability to hear a particular dispute. This depends on many things, including the type of dispute, the dollar amount contested, where the dispute arose, and the citizenship of the parties.

LESSEE—The person who rents real property, such as an apartment or house, or personal property, such as a car or home furnishings.

LESSOR—The person who owns and rents out to another any form of real property, such as an apartment or house, or personal property, such as a car or home furnishings.

LEVY—The act of getting the property of a debtor, typically after a judgment.

LIABILITY—Whether someone actually owes you money under the law for their actions or nonactions.

LIEN—An obligation which hangs over property until the judgment is paid off.

LIEN ON REAL ESTATE—A document which is either automatically or manually filed with the clerk stating that a person is indebted to you for a certain amount of money. The property cannot be sold until the lien is first paid off.

MECHANIC'S LIEN—A claim which secures payment for services or goods provided for the construction of a building by legally attaching a claim to the property.

NEGLIGENCE—Whether the actions of someone are wrong in the eyes of the law and they are responsible.

NSF—Nonsufficient funds. Typically, bank account is lacking available funds for a check to be accepted.

PERSONAL PROPERTY—Any property other than real estate.

PLAINTIFF—The person doing the suing.

PLEADING—Another name for the documents filed with the court.

PRIVATE PROCESS SERVER—A person specially appointed by the court to deliver court documents to parties to the case.

REAL PROPERTY—Real estate.

REPLEVIN—An action to recover personal property wrongfully held.

RULE TO SHOW CAUSE—Also called a contempt proceeding. (See Contempt.)

SECURED DEBT—Any obligation guaranteed by collateral of either real or personal property.

SERVICE OF PROCESS—The act of delivering the court documents to the other party in the action. This may be by certified mail, sheriff, or a private process server.

SKIPTRACING—tracing the steps of a debtor to determine their whereabouts and property.

SMALL CLAIMS—A special department in the courthouse which deals exclusively with small civil actions, typically below $5,000.

STATEMENT OF CLAIM—Synonymous with complaint. (See Complaint.)

STATUTE OF LIMITATIONS—The time period allowed by the state law as to the maximum time allowed between the time a debtor fails to pay you money and the time you sue him.

SUBPOENA—A court document typically delivered by the sheriff demanding a person to appear before the court at a certain date and time.

THEORY OF THE CASE—An explanation of what happened to cause the problem between the plaintiff and the defendant. The explanation of why it is that the plaintiff thinks the defendant owes the money. Each side has his own story, or theory of the case.

TRIAL—A more formal hearing. You will be expected to have your witnesses, testimony, and other evidence in order for this court appearance.

UNSECURED DEBT—An obligation not guaranteed by any form of collateral.

VENUE—The proper court(s) (or forum) where you can sue an individual or business.

WAGE GARNISHMENT—Used after a judgment is received. The creditor can use this to attach a percentage of the debtor's wages for a certain time period or until the judgment is paid off.

WITNESS—A person who is familiar with the history of your case who is brought to court to be examined by the judge.

WRIT OF EXECUTION—Used after a judgment is received. A document which is prepared by you, filed with the clerk, and given to the sheriff to serve on the defendant. It is an order to the sheriff to pick up certain property or possessions of the defendant and hand them over to you or sell them at a Sheriff's Auction and give you the proceeds.

Index

A

B

Index

C

D

E

Index

Index

U

V

W

Would You Like to Be In Our Next Book?

We're compiling a series of books that feature the best small business ideas. These can be ideas to save money, make money, motivate employees, increase sales, market your service, take care of your equipment needs, finance your business, collect money from creditors, negotiate a lease, improve customer service, develop team management, recruit new employees, develop new products, manage your sales force…in short, *ideas that really made a difference to the way you successfully run your business.* **We'd love to include your ideas!** We will, of course, give you credit for any ideas we publish. *Submissions become the property of the publisher.*

Please send your suggestions on your letterhead to:

Attn: "New Ideas" Dept.
Small Business Sourcebooks Series
P.O. Box 372
Naperville, IL 60566

Please be sure to include your name, address, phone number, FAX number if you have one and any pertinent information about your business (for example, a description of your business, the number of employees, your position). And again,
Thank You for working with Sourcebooks.

A Note from the Publisher

Hello!

I'm Dominique Raccah, head of Sourcebooks, Inc. In our business book series we've tried to bring you easy-to-use material to help you improve your key business skills. We've developed this series, with the help of a lot of entrepreneurs like yourself, to tackle some of the more common problems in building a business. As updated editions of these books are published, your input will be invaluable.

Please take the time to jot down any ideas you may have about the books you are using:

- Was the book useful?
- What would you like more of? What would you like less of?
- What else should be in this series?
- What are the most difficult areas facing you as you grow your business?

Please make sure you tell us which book you were using at the time. And please include your name, address and phone number so we can let you know if we incorporate your suggestions.

Thank You For Your Time and Your Support.

With Best Regards,

Dominique Raccah
and the staff of

Sourcebooks, Inc.
Small Business Sourcebooks
P.O. Box 372
Naperville, IL 60566
(708) 961-3900 FAX: (708) 961-2168

Do You Service Small Business Clients Too?

We, at Sourcebooks, have developed our business book program to serve the needs of the small business community. We've gotten incredible response to this series. If you are an accountant, lawyer, banker or consultant who also serves the small business community and you think our books could be of use to your clients, please give us a call. We offer special discounts to people who purchase these books to give or sell to their clients. Please contact us at 708-961-3900 or write to us at the address listed above for details. We'd love to work with you.